To anyone who finds my journal:

This is the story of how the War Between the States came to Comfort, Texas, in 1862. And how we Germans living here were called traitors for siding with the North—including my papa who refused to keep his opinions to himself. Everyone knows what happens to traitors. So I must find a way to save our family.

Anna Sophie Franziska Guenther

Sophie's War

The Journal of
Anna Sophie Franziska Guenther

Janice Shefelman

Illustrated by
Tom Shefelman

EAKIN PRESS ◆ Fort Worth, Texas
www.EakinPress.com

A note to the reader:
If you need help with German words,
look on pages 242-243.

Edited by Melissa Roberts
Designed by Virginia Messer,
Pat Molenaar,
and the Shefelmans

Copyright © 2006
By Janice Shefelman
Published By Eakin Press
An Imprint of Wild Horse Media Group
P.O. Box 331779
Fort Worth, Texas 76163
1-817-344-7036
www.EakinPress.com
ALL RIGHTS RESERVED
1 2 3 4 5 6 7 8 9
ISBN-10: 1-57168-880-3
ISBN-13: 978-1-57168-880-4
Library of Congress Control Number 2006924102

Comfort, Texas

1861 to 1862

Christmas Eve, 1861

Dear Reader,

I am afraid for us.

Terrible things are happening to Germans like us because we are on the wrong side of the war. We are Unionists in a state that has left the Union and joined the Confederacy.

What an awful way to begin my new journal—especially on Christmas Eve, the time of peace on earth and good will to men. But I have promised myself to write only the truth here.

This Christmas there is no peace and good will. There is a war going on, the war between the states, between the North and South. I don't mean that battles are being fought here in Texas—not yet anyway. But I have read stories in the newspaper about Germans being hanged for their belief in saving the Union.

By Union I mean the United States. We Germans want this country to stay together. But the southern states seceded and formed the Confederacy. Now only the North is called the Union. And we are killing each other to decide whether we are one country or two.

1

So I worry whenever Papa is late coming home, like tonight. He had gone on a hauling trip for Faltin Mercantile Store. I tried to forget my worries while I hung ornaments on the cedar tree. Still, I listened for Max, our sheepdog. He always makes happy yelps when Papa is coming. All I heard was the sizzling fire in the fireplace and Mama talking to Willie in the kitchen.

"Put the forks on the left, *Liebchen*," she said.

Setting the table is a girl's task, but Willie doesn't know. He is only three years old. The door between us was closed so he could not see the Christmas tree until after supper.

I took the glass strawberry out of the box. Last Christmas it came from *Grossmutter*, my grandmother who lives in Germany. This year we did not get a package from her because President Lincoln has ordered a blockade of our Gulf ports.

I hung the strawberry and started worrying about Papa again. What if the Vigilance Committee waylaid him? I thought if I went out on the gallery to watch, he would come. So I took my woolen shawl from the hook beside the door and stepped out. Wonder of wonders! Snow was falling! Never in the twelve years that we have lived in Texas has it snowed on Christmas Eve. Big flakes floated down, covering Mama's flower garden and the paths. Nothing evil could happen on such a magical night.

Max came to me and licked my fingers. I knelt to stroke his black fur, the white around his neck, and the blaze down his nose. Suddenly, his ears pricked. He lifted his nose, sniffing the air, and with a yelp bounded off toward the side gate. I knew it was Papa. Draping the shawl over my head, I followed Max and opened the gate. Together we ran down the road toward Cypress Creek.

And then I saw him through the white veil. He walked beside the two oxen as they pulled the wagon up the hill—his head high, his back straight. A sprinkling of snow lay across the broad shoulders of his coat and on his hat.

"Papa!" I called. "You're home! I was getting worried."

"*Ja, kleine* Sophie." He is the only one who can call me little Sophie.

When I reached him, he put one arm around my shoulders, and I fell into step while Max jumped all around us, yelping for joy. Papa smelled of cold, fresh air. I looked up at him and let the flakes land on my face. He is a tall, handsome man, my papa. Everyone says I favor him. We both have dark, curly hair, dimples, and a widow's peak. He does not wear a beard, but no one would take him for a boy.

"How are Willie and your mother?"

"They are both well, Papa." I knew he was

concerned about Mama because she is with child. "How was your trip? Did you sell any paintings?"

"Only two—Cypress Cathedral and Sheep Safely Grazing. San Antonio is not exactly Dresden."

I ran ahead to open the wagon gate, and Papa turned off the road. As we headed toward the barn, the front door opened, and Willie darted out, squealing about Papa and the snow.

Mama was behind him, her blonde hair braided and wrapped around her head like a halo. "Friedrich!" she called.

Papa strode through the garden gate, swept Willie up, and enclosed the two of them in his arms.

"Where is the *Weihnachtsmann*?" Willie asked. That is what we call Santa Claus.

"He's coming yet, Willie. Now, go inside before you catch cold—and don't look at the tree!" Papa set him down and started for the barn with Max at his heels. Then he turned. "Bring a lantern, will you, Sophie?"

By the time I got to the barn, Papa had driven the wagon into the passageway. I hung the lantern on a hook and closed the barn doors. While he removed the yoke I put some hay in the manger for the oxen.

Then Papa climbed into the wagon, ducked under the canvas cover, and handed me a large bag of oranges. I embraced it, inhaling the tangy smell.

"It wouldn't be Christmas without oranges,"

I said. Papa smiled, but I sensed that there was something on his mind. "What's wrong?" I asked.

He chuckled. "Nothing escapes you, does it, Sophie?"

"*Nein ...*" I replied, waiting.

"I think you should know about this, but you must not speak a word to your mother."

I shook my head, dreading what was to come.

"On the way home I passed by a German farmstead. The house had been burned to the ground, and the owner hung from a tree out front."

I gasped. "Why, Papa?" But I knew why.

"For being a Unionist, Sophie. For wanting to save the Union."

I could not speak for a moment. We could be next. Papa draws newspaper cartoons that criticize the Confederacy.

"Was it the Vigilance Committee?" I asked.

He nodded.

"Oh, Papa, please, I beg you ... don't speak out anymore! At least don't send cartoons to the *Zeitung*. Couldn't you just pretend to be for the Confederacy?"

He shook his head. "*Nein,* Sophie. I'll not pretend. I'll not condone slavery."

"But couldn't you just keep your thoughts to yourself?"

Papa stepped near and clasped my shoulders.

"Sophie, that is why we left Germany—so we could be free to say what we think. *Ja?*"

I said nothing.

He looked at me for a moment. "A man is not a man if he cannot speak his mind."

"I know, Papa. He is a dead man surely." I clapped my hand over my mouth. What if saying makes it so?

Papa's arms dropped to his side, and he took a step back.

"There are things worse than death, Sophie."

"What? What could possibly be worse?"

"Not being true to oneself."

"I don't care about that! I don't care about slaves or the Union. I don't want the war to come here. I don't want anything to change or . . . or die. Not ever, ever, ever!" There was a hard lump in my throat that would not go away even when I swallowed. And though I blinked to keep back the tears, they ran down my cheeks.

Papa took out his linen handkerchief. "Here, Sophie, wipe your eyes."

We stood in silence for a time. The only sound came from the oxen eating. I kept the handkerchief over my face.

"Sophie," Papa said at last, "everything does change whether you want it to or not. Everything that is alive grows and changes."

I looked at him. "And dies!"

"Sophie, you will grow into a young woman and marry and have children of your own, my grandchildren—perhaps another *kleine* Sophie."

"But how am I to get another papa?" I screamed, then turned and ran out of the barn, through the snow, to the house. I burst into the living room, dropped my shawl on the sofa, and began to decorate the tree, furiously. As I worked, the strawberry fell to the floor and shattered.

"*Ach, nein!*" I said, staring at the pieces.

Mama opened the kitchen door a crack. "Sophie, what did you break?"

I told her and began to sweep it up. My beloved strawberry was gone. Luck and glass—how easily they break. And all because of this dreadful war.

In the beginning I thought we were safe in our valley of the Guadalupe River with hills all around. The *San Antonio Zeitung* had stories about battles in faraway places like Virginia and South Carolina. But now the war is coming closer. You might say it is my war because it started this year on April 12, my twelfth birthday. Even so, what can I do about it? I'm just a young girl.

Soon Papa was stomping the snow off his boots out on the gallery. From the corner of my eye I saw him come in and set a bag on the floor by the tree.

"The *Weihnachtsmann* left this outside," he said. "You had better go in the kitchen while I put the gifts under the tree. I'll finish the decorating."

He hung his coat on a chair before the fire and stood there a moment with his back to me, warming his hands. In his brown waistcoat, his shoulders looked so broad and strong that suddenly I felt safe. Papa was home.

Turning around he said, "One last word, Sophie. Let's not waste the moment at hand for fear of the future. Or, as the Romans would say, *carpe diem* . . . seize the day."

I like to hear Papa speak Latin. It has a noble sound.

"Now, off you go, Sophie, and get my supper ready," he said. "I'm surely starving!"

Earlier Mama and I prepared herring salad, sweet potatoes, and ambrosia. The kitchen table was draped with a dark green cloth and set with our Meissen plates. In the center stood a white swan bowl filled with pansies from our garden.

Mama was in the bedroom changing Willie's dress. Papa will be glad when Willie is old enough to wear trousers. I think Mama does not want to admit that he is no longer her baby boy.

In a moment Papa opened the door and closed it quickly behind him. While he rubbed his hands over the cooking stove, Willie and Mama came into the kitchen. She had changed into her red silk Christmas dress. It lent her face a glow. Or maybe it was Papa's homecoming. I hope so.

All during supper Willie kept looking at the door to the living room. He swung his legs and scarcely ate anything.

"The *Weihnachtsmann* surely does not visit little boys until they finish supper," Mama said, which prompted Willie to eat a few bites.

At last Papa said, "I'll see if he has come, Willie."

Presently we heard the little brass bell ring, and Willie squealed, "He's come, he's come!"

Papa opened the door, and we all gasped. Our tree glowed with candles. Though the strawberry was gone, the orange and apple ornaments sparkled in the candlelight. Cookies hung, waiting to be plucked and eaten. Under the tree and in its branches lay gifts.

Willie stood looking at the tree. "A little horse!" he said and started toward it.

Mama took his hand. "*Ja, Liebchen,* but first we sing, remember?" She led him to the piano in the far corner. Willie climbed up on the bench beside her. Mama rubbed her hands together a moment and began to play. We sang "O *Tannenbaum,*" even though our tree was a cedar, and *Tannenbaum* means fir tree.

"O *Tannenbaum*, O *Tannenbaum*,
How faithful are your branches.
Not only green in summertime,
But also in freezing wintertime ..."

Outside the wind gusted against our log and stone house but could not get in. We were snug and safe—at least for now. And according to Papa, that is all that matters.

As soon as we finished singing, Willie rushed to the tree and reached for the little horse. Only then did he see a wooden man with yellow hair straddling a branch above. He took both and sat on the rug before the fire, intent on fitting the man on his horse.

Beneath the tree lay a small leatherbound book with a cover of blue marbled paper.

"For you, Sophie," Papa said. "The *Weihnachts-mann* brought it all the way from Venice."

I picked it up and ran my hand over the cover. "How beautiful!" I opened it and turned through the blank pages. "A journal!" I looked at Papa. "How could the *Weihnachtsmann* know this is the very thing I wanted most?"

"He knows everything," Willie said.

"You are right, Willie Boy," said Papa and turned back to me. "If you want to be a writer, Sophie, keeping a journal is as important as an artist keeping a sketchbook."

"I'll start it tonight, Papa."

For Mama there was a black silk shawl printed with red roses. Papa draped it around her shoulders. She looked down at the shawl, smiling, and then up at Papa.

If only they were always so loving. It seems there is a strange war in our household. Mama does not like Texas and wants to go back to Dresden. But Papa could not go back even if he wanted to, because he would be put in prison—or worse.

Later, after Papa banked the fire, I took my journal and a candle and climbed the stairs to the half story where Papa has his studio and I have my room under the eaves. I put on my nightdress, robe, and slippers. With a blanket wrapped around me I sit at my writing table in front of the window and dip my quill in the ink bottle.

I will write this journal like a novel, with the words people say as best as I can remember them. The book will be called *Sophie's War*, because I have a feeling that the coming year will be about the war. And I will write only when I have something significant to record.

Outside the snow swirls, piling even higher on the branches of the peach trees. In here I am safe and warm, separated from the rest of the world by the falling snow.

But tomorrow, who can say?

11

Wednesday,
February 19, 1862

On this sunny afternoon I am sitting in the liveoak that grows at the corner of our gallery. One trunk leans out from the house, so I walk partway up, climb onto a branch, and sit. From here I can look out across the meadow where our flock of sheep are grazing. The meadow slopes down to the edge of our cornfield. Beyond the field is Cypress Creek and beyond that, Comfort, our village.

In the opposite direction I can look down on the cypress shingles of our roof. Our house began as a small log cabin, chinked with stone and mortar. Then Papa added a living room and enclosed the back gallery with stone and half timbers. *Fachwerk*, we Germans call it.

I shall draw a plan for you, dear reader, and leave room for Papa to draw the house:

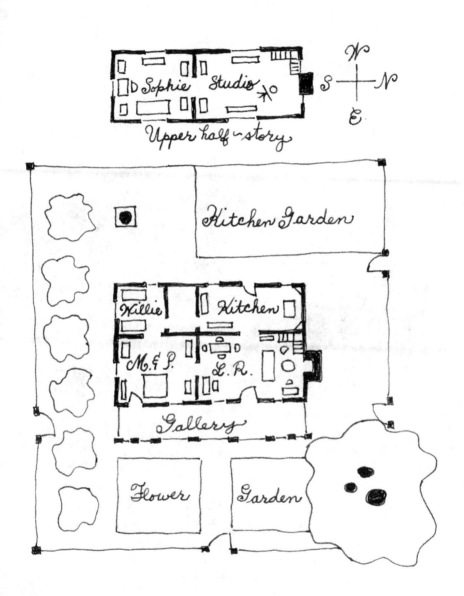

Sophie Studio

Upper half-story

N S N E

Kitchen Garden

Willie Kitchen

M.&P. L.R.

Gallery

Flower Garden

Now, a little about my life so far. My full name is Anna Sophie Franziska Guenther. Anna is for *Grossmutter*. Sophie is for novelist Sophie von Laroche— that was Papa's idea. He says, "I knew you were destined be a writer, because on the first day of your life you looked closely at everything." Franziska is for the ship that brought us here.

I was born in Dresden, capital of Saxony in Germany. All I know of the city is from a painting that Papa did as a student at the Academy of Fine Arts. When I was just a few months old, he took part in a demonstration against the king. There was fighting in the streets, but soldiers put a stop to it and arrested many people. Fortunately Papa escaped, and we left for Texas with a lot of other Germans.

For a time we lived in New Braunfels. When I was five years old our friend, Ernst Altgelt, started a settlement of Freethinkers here in the valley of the Guadalupe River, and we joined them. Being a Freethinker means we think for ourselves, without the help of a clergyman.

Later

Here is Papa's cartoon from last week's newspaper. I just hope no one in the Vigilance Committee saw it. The thought terrifies me, but Papa is determined to say what he thinks.

16

Can I change his mind and keep him safe? Somebody has to do it, and Mama cannot. They just get into an argument. So I resolved to try, beginning tonight at a meeting of the village militia in the schoolhouse.

After supper Papa went out to the barn. I opened the front door quietly, so Mama would not hear, and followed him. A crescent moon hung in the west like a white bowl waiting to catch Venus. I stopped to stare. Such a sight makes me wonder how men can kill each other down here on earth.

By the time I reached the barn, Papa was inside, hanging the lantern.

"May I go with you once, Papa?"

He turned to me with a look of amusement. "*Ja*, if your mother doesn't object, and you use your new sidesaddle."

Even though I hate the sidesaddle, I nodded, picked up my skirts, and ran back to the house. Mama was putting Willie to bed.

"Papa asked me to go to the meeting with him," I said.

The line between her brows deepened, and she blinked several times. "Young ladies do not go to public meetings. Certainly I never did."

"*Tante* Emma does. I could sit with her."

17

"You are not Emma Altgelt," Mama said. "Anyway, why would you want to hear all that war talk?"

I could not tell her that I was afraid for Papa. Not in her condition.

Willie sat up in bed, looking from one of us to the other. "No fighting." That is what he calls arguing.

Mama laughed and cupped his face in her hands. "*Nein, Liebchen*, no fighting. Now, time to go to sleep."

He lay back on his pillow.

She sighed and looked at me. "Well, perhaps it is a good idea. With you there, your father will be more careful of what he says."

"That's what I thought."

I kissed Willie and hurried out to the barn.

Papa had already saddled Pegasus, my pure white horse. With Papa on Bucephalus, we rode out, down the road, and splashed through the creek. Peg kept turning his head around to see why my legs were both on one side. He doesn't like the sidesaddle either.

We trotted along Broadway, which is nothing like the Broadway in New York City. I've heard that it is lined with buildings that are four and five stories high. In Comfort we only have a few scattered log houses and the schoolhouse.

After tying our horses to a fence post in front of the school, Papa opened the gate for me. Lamplight streamed out the open door, and so did the scent of pipe tobacco. Inside thirty or forty men sat on our school benches or stood against the wall. At the front of the room, *Herr* Heuermann sat at our teacher's desk, which seemed odd since he is so much larger than *Herr* Steves.

Papa motioned me to a bench along the side wall where *Tante* Emma was sitting—the only woman. She smiled and patted a place beside her. I have always called her *Tante*, which means aunt, because she is Mama's friend. She is slender and, in a way, still a girl. Her mother and a female slave take care of the household while she goes everywhere with her husband.

"I am surprised your mother let you come, Sophie."

"It's because she thinks my being here might keep Papa from saying things he shouldn't."

"So," she said, nodding. "Tell me, have you written any more poems lately?"

"Not lately, but I've started a journal."

"*Gut*," she said. "You know, I once dreamed of being a writer, but I gave it all up for my dashing cavalier." She meant her husband.

Right then I promised myself that I would never give up writing for anyone. Not even Eduard Meyer who is fifteen and never notices me anyway. He probably thinks I am too young for him. I looked around to see if he was there. And he was, standing at the back of the room, so tall and manly. My heart gave a little leap. *Ja*, I am in love with Eduard. With a papa like mine, how could I fall for less?

Papa took a seat on the end of the bench in front of me. Behind him sat James Boyd and his son Thomas. They live south of town, across the Guadalupe. Here in Comfort we are all Germans, and the men were all educated in German universities. But we are surrounded by a sea of rabble, as Mama calls Texans. Rebel rabble, I call them.

Herr Heuermann tapped his pipe on the desk to call the meeting to order. Then he began in his deep voice.

"We gather this evening to record the firearms we have among us and to determine how we can protect our homes and families. As everyone knows, Union troops have abandoned Camp Verde and Fort Mason, leaving us at the mercy of redskins and Confederate ruffians." He leaned forward, elbows on the desk. "And in my opinion the ruffians are more to be feared."

At that moment Papa stood to speak and my heart sank. I glanced at Mister Boyd, wondering if he was one of those ruffians. He is a big, burly man with black hair.

"Papa," I whispered.

He glanced at me and I shook my head ever so slightly. But he paid me no mind.

"*Ja*, Wilhelm, you are right. But let us not fear

these ruffians or Vigilance Committee or whatever they call themselves. We must protect ourselves, of course, but we must not let them silence us." Papa paused and looked around the room. "Is that not why we left our fatherland? Have we come across the ocean only to be silenced by a group of ruffians? I say *nein!*"

Mister Boyd was looking at Papa with squinted eyes. *Ach*, he gives me the shivers!

"Like most of you, I believe in the Union, in the United States of America," Papa went on. "Not the Confederate States of America. I want no part of slavery and surely will not fight for it. But I will defend my family and anyone else threatened by these ruffians. So, please record that I, Friedrich Guenther, have a six-shooter, a five-shot pistol, and a rifle."

He sat down at last. Mama and I were wrong. My being there did nothing to restrain him. But it made me realize that I should ask Papa to teach me to fire his pistol.

On the front row *Herr* Altgelt, *Tante* Emma's husband, stood—her dashing cavalier in coat and cravat. "Like Friedrich, I will defend my family and our village with my firearms, a six-shooter and a shotgun." Then he turned to look at Papa. "I respect your beliefs about the Union, Friedrich, but I must disagree. I do not believe the Yankees have the right to tell us to abolish slavery. Every state has the right to decide that issue for itself. After all, there are great plantations that could not exist without slaves."

Why not? I wondered. Couldn't they just have hired help like our Arlis and Rosina? Why do they have to own people like sheep?

Herr Altgelt paused and made a courtly gesture to include everyone. "Nevertheless, though we may disagree, I say there are no traitors in this schoolhouse."

One by one the men stood and gave an account of their weapons, if not their views. At the end of the meeting *Herr* Heuermann suggested an alarm signal to call the militia together—one long blast on a cow's horn. Everyone agreed, even Mister Boyd. Still, I don't trust him.

On the way home I said, "I wish you would be more careful about what you say, Papa."

"We have already discussed that, Sophie."

"I know, but what if Mister Boyd is one of those ruffians—maybe even one of the Vigilance Committee?"

"You're imagining things. The man is just an uneducated bacon farmer."

I said no more. It did not seem like a good time to ask him to teach me to shoot. But I will do so, and soon. What if the Vigilance Committee comes while Papa is off on a hauling trip?

Thursday, March 6

Two things happened at school today that I must record. One made me realize how much I hate Thomas Boyd, the other how much I love Eduard Meyer. I will begin with Thomas.

Herr Steves lets us go outside to eat our dinner on nice days. I always eat with my friend Etta Lange, the only other twelve-year-old girl in our school. Her real name is Henrietta, which she hates. She says it sounds like a chicken! We have set up a box for a table and two logs for seats under a liveoak tree. The younger girls don't bother us anymore because Etta told them you had to be twelve to eat here. The older girls gather near the gymnastics bar where the boys are.

At noon today Etta and I went straight to our place. I began taking bread, cheese, sausage, a pickle, and cookies out of my dinner pail.

Etta looked toward the gymnastics bar. "Uh-oh, here comes big old Thomas Boyd."

I went on laying out my dinner, watching him from the corner of my eye.

"Don't worry," Etta whispered. "If he tries to come near us, I'll chase him off and kick his rear end."

I laughed out loud. She is such a *Wildfang!*

Thomas stopped about six feet away and put his hands on his hips. I looked up at him then. His thick, dark hair was uncombed and his shirt and trousers wrinkled. "I wouldn't be laughing if *my* papa was a Yankee lover," he said in English.

I kept my face composed, but my heart pounded. What could I say? I surely did not want to anger him and bring on a visit from a bunch of ruffians.

"Can't you talk English?" he asked.

He knows I can. We speak English in class.

Etta jumped up, flipped her reddish braids back, and put her hands on her hips too. "Sophie does not talk to bacon farmers!" she said in her best English.

Ach, she is going to get us killed one day. Indeed, Thomas shot a look at her that could, and then turned it back on me. I looked at my food and picked up a slice of cheese. I could feel his anger burning the side of my face.

"I'd rather be a bacon farmer than a traitor. That's what your papa is—a traitor." He spat the word at me.

I looked at him and bit my lips together to keep from shouting, *Your father is the traitor, not mine!* Then I turned away, for I could not bear the sight of his sneering face.

"You are a *Dummkopf!* Know what that means?" Etta said, sticking her chin out. "It means dumbhead."

He scowled. "And you want to be a boy."

"I do not!" Etta picked up her skirts and ran at him. She started punching him and kicking his shins. He put up his muscular arms in defense and pretended to beg. "Please, Miss Henrietta, don't hit me."

Eduard came striding toward them. "Hey, Thomas, leave her alone."

Just then *Herr* Steves appeared at the door of the schoolhouse. "What is going on out here? Thomas, are you causing trouble?"

"No, sir. Miss Henrietta was trying to kiss me."

"*Kick* is the word," Etta yelled.

Thomas threw back his head and laughed. Etta jabbed at him with her fist, but he ducked and ran off, still laughing.

Eduard looked at me and lifted his arms in a shrug, as if to say, *What can you expect of bacon farmers*? It was not much, but it made me forget about Thomas.

In the afternoon *Herr* Steves announced that we were going to read aloud from Schiller's play, *William Tell*, Act Three. "Eduard, you will read the part of Tell."

Of course, who else? I glanced at Eduard. He could be the son of gods—like Apollo, golden and tall and straight. His full name is Marc Antony Eduard Meyer. The first two names are for the Roman who fell in love with Cleopatra.

No one knows I like him, except you, dear reader. But he probably likes Christine. All the boys do because she has breasts. Etta calls her Christine the Beauty Queen. She is no Cleopatra though. It was not Cleopatra's beauty that attracted men like Antony and Caesar—it was her intelligence. So perhaps there is hope for me.

Still, I was startled when *Herr* Steves said, "And Sophie, you will read the part of Hedwig, Tell's wife."

I wanted to crawl under the bench. Was Eduard looking at me? Was he amused? Fortunately I had on my prettiest school dress, the pale green with ruffled sleeves.

Herr Steves assigned Etta to read the part of Walter, the son, Christine to read Berta, a rich heiress, Thomas to read a soldier's part, and himself to read Gessler, the governor. When all the parts were assigned, we began to read.

I dearly love Act Three. William Tell refuses to bow to the Swiss governor's hat that hangs on top of a pole. As punishment the governor forces Tell to shoot an apple from his son's head with his bow and arrow.

As I read I forgot myself and became Hedwig. She senses something evil is going to happen that day and begs her husband to stay at home. Here is part of what I read. It sounds like something Mama or I would say to Papa.

Hedwig:
But you are not concerned about my fears—
How I may worry, waiting here for you;
For I am terrified at what they tell
About your daring trips and risky ventures ...

Then Eduard read William Tell's answer. It could have been Papa talking.

Tell:
Whoever looks around with open eyes
And trusts in God and his own ready strength
Can keep himself from danger and distress.
He fears no mountains who was born among
    them.

I looked at Eduard when he finished reading those brave lines, and he looked at me. Something passed between us. I was playing his wife and he my husband, and for a moment it seemed real.

After school I went out and mounted Pegasus. Papa wanted me to come straight home and sit for a portrait. Just as I started off, Eduard approached. I thought my heart would leap out of my body! I pulled on Peg's reins.

"I enjoyed reading the play together," he said, looking up at me with his blue eyes. "You read with feeling."

I was stunned. "*Danke.* So do you."

"Father, Mother," Etta called as she ran toward us. "It's me, your brave son Walter." She stopped and looked at Eduard. "That was some shot, Father."

We all laughed.

"Well, *auf Wiedersehen,* Hedwig, Walter," Eduard said and mounted his horse.

After he left, Etta said, "He likes you, Sophie."

"How do you know?"

"Why else would he be talking to you?"

I shrugged, but I hope she is right. Maybe he likes my brain and knows that one day I will have breasts.

As Peg splashed across Cypress Creek on the way home, I looked at the gnarled cypress root that has an owl's face on it. At least that is what it looks like to me. I call him Old Man Owl. I think he knows about Eduard because one eye is winking like this:

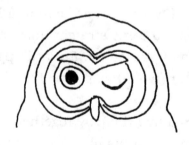

Then Pegasus and I started up the long, gentle slope to our house. Our cornfield had been plowed while I was at school. Papa always does his farm work in the morning, and in the afternoon he works in his studio—exercise for both the body and the mind. That is the way of Latin farmers, the name Texans gave us. They find it odd that we speak and read Latin. But now they find it odd that we are Unionists and call us traitors instead.

Willie and Rosina, our hired girl, were out gathering the laundry from the fence on the south side of our house. She is a big girl and strong of limb but not very strong of mind. Still, she loves us—especially Willie. I called to them and waved. Mama was sitting on the gallery. She has to take care now, for it is only a couple of months until the baby comes. Her full skirt can no longer hide the fact that she is with child. Of course, Willie knows nothing of a baby. Mama just tells him she has a fat stomach from putting too much butter on her cornbread.

After unsaddling Pegasus and turning him out, I climbed the stairs to Papa's studio. There are dormer windows in the roof, front and back, which let in air and light. Papa was pinning a piece of paper to his easel.

"Ah, Sophie, there you are. How was school today?"

I shrugged. "*Gut* and bad. The *gut* part is that *Herr* Steves had us read aloud from Act Three of *William Tell,* and I got to be Hedwig."

"And who was Tell?"

My face grew hot. "Eduard." I saw the amusement in Papa's eyes and looked away.

"Well, I am delighted that you are so fond of Schiller."

I heard the smile in his voice. There was a pause, and I pretended to study a painting of our homestead on the wall.

"So . . . what could be bad about such a day?" Papa went on.

I shook my head.

He studied me for a moment. Then he said, "*Alta flumina minimo sono labuntur.*"

"What does that mean?"

"It's a Roman proverb that literally means deep waters flow with little sound."

I smiled. "Meaning *me*?"

"*Ja-ja,* Sophie, meaning you." Papa pulled up a stool and motioned me to the chair beside his easel. He had me face the window, turn my head, and look at him. "Now that same little smile . . . just enough to show your dimples."

I stayed very still, holding the smile. The wind soughed in the liveoaks outside the window and sheep were bleating to each other in the distance.

Papa's pencil scraped on the paper. I forgot everything except Eduard.

After a time Papa put his pencil down, stepped back to look, and pronounced it *wunderbar!*

"Come see, Sophie."

I came and stood beside him. The girl in the drawing was beautiful. "Am I that pretty, Papa?"

"*Jawohl!* Yes, indeed," he said. "Now will you tell me what happened at school?"

I told him what Thomas had said.

"His calling me a traitor doesn't make it so," Papa said.

"It's not his words that worry me, Papa. It's what his father might do."

"Sophie, I can take care of myself and my family. No bacon farmer is going to tell me how to think or act."

"*Nein*, but what if you just thought and didn't act?"

"You know I can't do that, Sophie. It's my duty as a cartoonist to shine a light on evil, so to speak."

I sighed. There was no use trying to change my idealistic Papa. "Then will you teach me to fire your small pistol?"

"You are that afraid, Sophie?"

"*Ja*, and I've decided it's not enough to be afraid."

He looked at me for a moment and began nodding his head. "Tomorrow, after school. But not a word to your mother."

31

Friday, March 7

When I got home from school Papa had his horse saddled, and we rode up the hill behind our barn. He had told Mama that we were going to the upper pasture to see if one of our cows had birthed her calf.

"What if Mama hears gunshots? Won't that alarm her?"

"*Nein*, I told her I would try to bring back a deer." He chuckled. "That's why I brought my rifle as well."

After about a mile we came to a wide ravine.

"A good place," Papa said, dismounting. He got his gun case out of the saddlebag and opened it. Nestled inside were the pistol, a powder flask, lead balls, a tin of percussion caps, and another of lard. He picked up the pistol. "First, never point a gun at anything unless you plan to shoot."

I nodded.

He handed it to me. "Aim at that white rock on the other side of the ravine, Sophie. Pull the hammer back to full cock and get the front and rear sights lined up."

I held the pistol at arm's length and squinted one eye.

"*Gut*. When you're ready, slowly squeeze the trigger."

I squeezed. BLAM! The blast pitched my arm upward, and the shot hit the side of the ravine above the rock.

"Try both hands, Sophie. Make your arms like a triangle."

I gripped the handle with both hands, cocked the hammer, got a steady sight on the rock, and squeezed the trigger.

BLAM! A piece of the rock flew off.

I lowered the gun and looked at Papa.

He was nodding. "*Sehr gut.* You have the idea."

After I fired the remaining shots, shattering the rock, I handed the pistol back to him.

"Now for loading. Watch carefully." He held the gun muzzle-up and poured powder into an empty chamber. "First the powder, then the ball." He placed a lead ball on top of the powder and rotated the cylinder so that it lined up with the rammer. "Then you unlatch the rammer and press the ball into the chamber nice and tight." After he loaded one more chamber, he had me load the remaining three.

"Next comes the lard." He opened the tin and used a knife to spread a little lard over each ball. "This seals the chamber and keeps the flame from igniting others when you fire."

"*Gut* idea," I said, horrified at the thought.

"And last of all, the percussion caps—that's what ignites the powder and fires the ball."

As I watched Papa seat the caps on the nipples, I wondered if I could fire one of those deadly little balls into a person. At least I know how.

Now it is late, but I dip my quill and write on. Candlelight shines on the plank ceiling that slopes down on either side of me like a tent. This room is my sanctuary, a place for things I love. On the table stands a small woodcarving of a girl playing the violoncello. It is a music box, and when you wind it up she turns around to the tune of "You Live in My Heart, Dear."

My books are in a shelf tucked under the dormer window on the west wall. Under the east dormer stands my wooden bedstead with winged head and foot boards. And on the washstand beside the door are a flowery Meissen pitcher and basin.

As I write I can hear the call of a screech owl. It is such a sweet, quavering sound. I leaned toward the window to look out. *Ja*, there he is, a small dark shape in the peach tree. A full moon has risen and clouds are racing past it, headed north. Is Eduard watching it too?

Added later

Little did I know as I watched the moon that President Lincoln's son, named Willie like my brother, died of a fever this night. He was my age—a gentle boy who wrote poetry. Why Willie Lincoln instead of Thomas Boyd?

Friday, March 14

It was poetry day at school. *Herr* Steves asked us to choose a poem or write one to read aloud. Here is the one I wrote. *Herr* Steves praised the "imagery of my metaphor," as he put it.

> Cypress Cathedral
> There is a cathedral in Dresden
> That I have never seen,
> But it could not be as lovely
> As a cathedral of lacy green.
> Along the banks of Cypress Creek
> The trees are like a colonnade,
> Their branches spiraling high
> Above the water of luminous jade.

After school I went out by the fence to wait for Etta. She had to stay and look up a poem because she had forgotten to bring one. As I was untying Peg, Eduard strode over.

"I liked your poem. The words made pictures in my mind—especially 'Their branches spiraling high above the water of luminous jade.' That's beautiful."

I caught my breath. "*Danke*." For a moment I could not think what else to say. Then I remembered his reading of Marc Antony's speech from *Julius Caesar*. "And you made the schoolhouse seem like the Roman Forum."

He laughed. "*Danke.*"

"I always hope they won't kill Caesar, but they always do," I said.

"Me too. So you like Shakespeare?"

"*Ja.*"

"What is your favorite play?"

I hesitated. I did not dare say *Romeo and Juliet*. "It's hard to choose. What is yours?"

"*Hamlet*, I think. Or maybe *Julius Caesar.*"

"Papa is going to read aloud from *Julius Caesar* tonight for the Ides of March," I said.

He nodded. "Maybe I'll read it again too." He untied his horse and mounted. "So, *auf Wiedersehen.*"

He waved and started off toward his family's farm, which is on the other side of Comfort from ours. I mounted Pegasus and rode home too, forgetting all about Etta.

After supper Papa brought out *The Globe Illustrated Shakespeare* and laid it on the table. It is a thick book covered in red leather with gold-edged pages. He turned to the title page of the play where there is a woodcut illustration of Brutus, sword in hand, standing over the fallen Caesar.

While Mama knitted socks and Willie played with his wooden horse, Papa read. He uses a different voice for each part. In the beginning Caesar is walking with his attendants through the streets of Rome when an old soothsayer calls out to him.

Papa hunched his shoulders and looked at us from under his thick, dark eyebrows. "Beware the Ides of March," he said in a scratchy voice.

It made me shiver. If Papa had been the soothsayer, Caesar would have listened. Instead he calls the old man a dreamer. But the dream comes true, and Caesar is assassinated on that very day.

Later, after I had gone upstairs, Mama rushed in the back door from the *Häuschen*, the outhouse. "Friedrich, Indian fires!"

I ran through Papa's studio to the top of the stairs and looked out the north window. There were three signal fires high in the hills. I gasped, remembering that Papa planned to go looking for our cows tomorrow.

"Calm yourself, Elisabet," Papa said. "You mustn't get so upset in your condition. Here, sit down and I'll have a look around and make sure the barn is locked." Then he came into the living room, took down his rifle, and went out.

I rushed downstairs and caught up with him at the gate. "Papa, beware the Ides of March."

He threw back his head and laughed—the kind

of hearty laugh that usually makes me smile, but not this time. "Who do you think I am ... Julius Caesar?"

"*Nein,*" I said as we walked to the barn. "You are my papa and I don't want anything to happen to you."

"Don't worry, Sophie. The Comanches hate Texans, not Germans. We have a treaty with the Penateka band that has never been broken on either side."

I still couldn't help worrying, even though I knew about that treaty. Then I wondered ...

"How do they tell Germans from Texans?"

"We say *alemán*—German. Most of them understand a little Spanish." Papa tried the lock on the bolt, and we started back to the house. "I won't live in fear, Sophie. Anyway, most of the Indians in these parts are Penateka."

"Then I'll go with you. Please, Papa ... otherwise I'll just worry."

We paused outside the door.

"Are you sure you want to go?" he asked. "I may have to camp overnight."

Sleep out with only the sky for a roof and no walls to protect us? I took a deep breath. "I'm sure."

Mama was sitting in the kitchen with Willie on her lap.

"All is well, *meine Lieben,*" Papa said. "They are only looking for horses, and our barn is securely locked."

"How do you know what they intend, Friedrich?" Her voice had that sharp edge that cuts through me.

"Because I trust them to honor the treaty, Elisabet. Now, let's get some sleep. I'll be starting out early."

There was a stunned silence.

"You are going after the cows when there are Indians out there?" Mama said.

"They will move on at dawn."

Mama glanced up at the ceiling. "*Ach*, Friedrich, you can't know that for sure."

"No fighting," Willie said.

Mama and Papa looked at him, then at each other.

"Trust me, Elisabet."

She just blinked at him, her lips pressed together. I hate her when she looks at Papa that way.

"Don't be mad, Mama," said Willie. "Don't blink your eyes so fast." He raised his arms and put his plump little hands over her eyes.

In spite of herself, Mama laughed, took his hands in hers, and kissed them. "All right, Willie, no blinking . . . no fighting."

Later that night

After I finished writing I blew out the candle and climbed into my feather bed. For a long time I lay awake, looking up at the little square of starry sky through the window. The fires were not very far away. And what if the Indians were not Penateka?

When sleep came at last, I dreamed of an Indian peering in the window, his face hideous with war paint. He scratched on the glass with his fingernails.

I awoke and sat bolt upright. Something was surely scratching at the window, but it was not an Indian. It was a tree branch. I threw myself back on my pillows, my heart still thumping.

A long time ago when I first moved upstairs, branches of that same tree scraped on the window. I cried out for Papa, and he came bounding up to my room.

"What is it, *kleine* Sophie?" He sat down beside me.

When I told him there was something outside my window, he put his hand on my forehead and smoothed back my hair. "It's only the wind and the peach tree, nothing more." He went to the window and opened it. A breeze lifted the curtains. "You see? Only the wind." He came and sat beside me again. "Now, go to sleep. All is well."

Remembering made me feel safe now. That is why I crept downstairs, lit the candle, and wrote these last words.

Saturday, March 15
The Ides of March

In the morning after breakfast, Papa and I went out to saddle our horses. He did not even give me a look when I put my old saddle on Pegasus instead of the sidesaddle. Maybe he decided if I was going to do a man's work, I could ride like a man. Peg tossed his *milch*-white head and pranced. It is easy to see why Indians would want to steal him.

We led our horses to the side gate, where Mama and Willie stood waiting. Mama handed me a parcel of food tied in a cloth. Papa hugged her while I gave Willie a kiss and ruffled his hair. Max whined, wagging his tail at the same time. He could not understand why he was not going for the cows.

"Take care of them, Max," Papa said.

Birds were announcing the sunrise: cardinals chirped, and a mockingbird sat in the yaupon tree, singing. A good sign. If the mockingbird is sitting in that tree when I leave the house, all will go well. If not, beware.

Papa and I mounted and made our way through the herd of sheep with their baby lambs. Bells tinkled as they scattered. We rode past the barn and up the rise and then turned and waved to Mama and Willie.

The liveoak branches are beginning to bud in spite of the drought. There has been no rain for six months, only the light snowfall at Christmas. Papa says there may not be any bluebonnets this year.

All morning we rode to the northwest, zigzagging between Cypress and Wilson creeks. We saw only two cows and their calves that belonged to our neighbor. But in the afternoon we came upon one of our cows chewing her cud while a new calf suckled.

"We'll leave them and come back after we find the others," Papa said.

Finally, in a broad meadow, we spied the rest of our cattle. Since it was too late to drive them home, we found a good place to camp under a spreading liveoak. The sun had already sunk below the hills, and darkness was coming on fast. More than anything I wanted a fire.

"I'll go and gather some wood," I said.

"*Nein*, Sophie, no fire tonight."

"Why, Papa? It would keep the dark away."

"It's the Indians I want to keep away."

I felt a stab of alarm but said nothing.

Later, after we had eaten some bread and *Kochkäse*, we spread our blankets. As I lay looking

43

up at the stars, I found the three that form Orion's belt.

"There's Orion, Papa."

"*Ja*, I see it. Did you know Orion was called Osiris by the ancient Egyptians?"

"Who was Osiris?" I asked.

"God of the underworld."

"In the sky?"

"Well, you see, Sophie, in the universe there is no over and under, no then and now. Not even a beginning or end."

"I can't understand that, Papa."

"Neither can I, but we are meant to try."

After a moment I said, "It's so big—the universe."

"*Ja*, endless."

"It makes me feel very small."

"We *are* small, Sophie. But our minds are big . . . big enough to glimpse the mystery of the universe."

"What is the mystery of the universe?"

Papa chuckled. "If we knew for sure, it wouldn't be a mystery. But I think it's the way we are all connected into One."

"Is that One what *Gott* is?"

"Perhaps. But you must read and think on it. The worst thing is to let someone put a metal band around your head so new ideas can't get in."

"A metal band?"

"I mean that metaphorically, Sophie. The metal band of the church."

"Ah, now I understand."

Sometime during the night a norther blew in. The wind soughed in the branches overhead, making a lonely sound. I awoke to find another blanket covering me.

Sunday, March 16

At first light I heard Papa stirring and poked my head out from under the blankets.

"No fire this morning either," he said. "The wind is too strong, and everything is too dry."

We started home then, Papa on one side of the herd and I on the other. It was overcast, and the wind cut through my heavy cloak. The calves stayed close by their mothers for warmth. When we got back to the place where we had seen our first cow and calf, they were gone.

"Maybe they crossed the creek," Papa said. "I'll go and have a look. You stay here with the herd." He handed me his small pistol.

My heart jumped. I knew that he was worried about Indians.

"Just fire one shot in the air if you need me," he said.

I nodded and watched him ride off. Then I stuck the pistol in my belt and wrapped my cloak around me. After a time, Peg pulled on his reins. He wanted water, so we started down to the creek. Halfway there he stopped, raised his head, and sniffed the air. It was then that I heard a sound that set my heart pounding—the call of an owl.

Peg's ears pricked. Ordinarily this sound would not alarm either of us, but there was something odd about it. Was it an owl or an Indian?

I pulled the pistol from my belt and cocked the hammer. Suddenly, an Indian came riding out from behind the underbrush upstream. Peg reared. Clutching the saddle horn with one hand, I fired a shot in the air. The Indian pulled up his horse perhaps ten feet away.

I wondered if I dared race for the creek. Was another one waiting there? Were they Penateka? Then I remembered what Papa said.

"*Alemán!*" I shouted, giving Peg a kick.

The Indian held up two fingers, the sign for friend, and I glimpsed his face as we galloped by. Good old Pegasus—he flew across the creek and through the underbrush as if he truly had wings. I just let him go, and all at once there was Papa. I pulled on the reins and jumped off.

Papa's arms enclosed me. "Sophie, Sophie . . . what happened?"

"An Indian . . .!" I was short of breath and could say no more for a moment.

"Did he . . . did he . . . harm you?"

I shook my head and stepped back until I could

catch my breath. "No, Papa. When I yelled *alemán* he made the sign for friend. I think he only wanted Pegasus, and when he realized I was German he changed his mind."

"Well, if you are all right I intend to take him at his word." He held out his hand. "May I have the pistol?" I was still clutching it at my side but gave it to him. "Now, let's go back for the strays. I found them almost to North Creek." He stuck the pistol in his holster. "Not a word of this to your mother."

"*Nein*, Papa."

As we rode along, the scene played over in my mind. I saw the Indian clearly now, mounted on his red horse, silver breastplate glinting on his chest. His face looked intelligent, even gentle.

"Why do you think he came here, Papa?"

"For horses, especially a white one. Indians consider them sacred."

"I caught only a glimpse of his face, but I don't think he was going to harm me. Even if he did want to steal Pegasus."

"I think you're right." He looked over at me and chuckled. "*Ja*, Sophie, you've had quite an adventure. And you rose to the occasion."

"How so, Papa?"

"You looked around with open eyes and kept yourself from danger—just like William Tell. And you said the important word, *alemán*. Don't ever forget it."

"*Nein*, Papa." I smiled to myself at his praise. "I think I'm about five years older now."

When we got home, Mama met us at the door with Willie holding on to her skirt.

"Friedrich, I want to leave this savage place. I want to go back to Dresden now! If it's not the war, it's Indians."

"What, Elisabet? What happened?"

"Indians . . . two of them down by the creek."

"Did they come to the house?" Papa asked.

"*Nein*, but they could have. And you out hunting cows!"

Papa strode to her, taking her in his arms, but she threw them off.

"No fighting," Willie cried, but no one listened.

"I don't know why I ever let you bring me here. I hate living on the edge of nowhere. I hate this log cabin. I want to live in a real house in Dresden." She started to sob and finally let Papa take her in his arms.

I picked up Willie and held him, even though he reached for Mama.

"Elisabet, you surely know we can't go back now. You mustn't get yourself all worked up." He led her toward their sleeping room. "I promise to think about

49

it, *meine Liebe*, if only you will be calm. Come, now. Lie down on the bed."

Willie watched them with his finger in his mouth, taking jerky little breaths.

"It will be all right, Willie," I whispered. "Come, help me fix supper. You can set the table."

After Willie was in bed, I sat at the dining table writing in my journal. Mama was playing a song by Schumann while Papa stood beside her, singing of a poet's love.

There seems to be a truce in our strange war.

Friday, April 11

Tomorrow the war will be one year old, and I will be thirteen. I'm catching up with Eduard. He is still only fifteen! Usually it is a lovely time to have a birthday, with bluebonnets and Indian paintbrush covering the meadows. This year, though, we have a drought and a war. All I want for my birthday is for the war to end, but I am afraid it is getting worse.

General Albert Sidney Johnston, a Texan, was killed by Union forces at a place called Shiloh in Tennessee. He bled to death under a peach tree covered with pink blossoms. How can men shoot at each other in a peach orchard? Now Texans will hate us German Unionists even more because we are on the side that killed their beloved general.

I decided to talk to Papa again.

After school I went straight upstairs. Papa sat at his drawing board with his back to me. When he is at work he neither sees nor hears anything else. I looked over his shoulder, and my heart sank. He was drawing a cartoon for the *Zeitung* about the death of General Johnston.

I stood behind him, scarcely breathing. This one was going to get him in trouble. I had to do something, and begging did not seem to work. Suddenly, I knew I had to destroy the cartoon. The very thought made my heart pound.

Papa must have heard it, for he turned to look at me. I reached for the cartoon, snatched it from the drawing board, and stepped back. I tore it in half as he stared at me in disbelief.

"You can't send this cartoon to the newspaper, Papa. Texans love General Johnston. I'm afraid the Vigilance Committee will come after you."

Papa laid down his pen and stood. "I have been patient with your fears, Sophie, but this is going too far." He reached out his hand. "Now, give it back."

I shook my head.

"Sophie, do you want to let the Vigilance Committee rule the world? If so, go ahead, tear the cartoon into a thousand little pieces, and I'll cower at their feet. Is that what you want—a coward for a father?"

I shook my head. Oh, what did I want?

"Do you think I'm not afraid too?" Papa asked.

"I don't know, Papa. Aren't you like William Tell?"

"I try to be, but he was afraid when he was forced to shoot an apple from his son's head. Remember how his arm trembled?"

"I remember."

"But he did what he had to do. And I will do no

less, even if I have to draw the cartoon again. In times like these we all have to do what we are afraid to do."

I looked down at the two pieces of the cartoon in my hands and felt my face twist at the sight. "Oh, Papa, what have I done?"

"It can be pasted together," he said. "That's easier than your task."

How true. Much as I hate the cartoon, I will leave room here for it so that you, dear reader, can understand why I am afraid for us.

THE DEATH OF GENERAL JOHNSTON

Saturday, April 12
My Birthday

I believe that whatever you do on your birthday—
like getting up early, making yourself pretty, doing
your chores happily, and trying to be brave—foretells
how you will be for the next year.

So I got up at dawn and looked out my window.
The sky was growing pink behind the dark cypress
trees along the creek. In our cornfield I could see
the green shoots that had come up in spite of the
drought. I watched until the tip of the sun flashed
between the branches. My day had begun. It would
be the strangest birthday ever.

I poured water into the basin and washed. After
I put on clean drawers, chemise, and petticoats, I
slipped into my pale green dress. Then I parted my
hair down the middle and tied back my curls on
either side with ribbons that match the dress. I
smiled at my reflection in the looking glass.

As I walked through Papa's studio, I saw that
he had already repaired the cartoon. The tear was
scarcely visible—not that it mattered. The engraver
would redraw it on a wood block anyway. Papa will

send it with the next week's mail, and I won't try to stop him again. I surely do not want him to be a coward. Nor do I want him to be hanged. What, then?

Downstairs Willie rushed out of the kitchen and flung himself at me on his stubby little legs, squealing, "Happy birthday, Sophie!"

I hugged him. "Do you know how old I am?"

He shook his head. "How old?"

"Thirteen. Can you count that far?"

He nodded and began, but at ten he needed help.

Mama came out of the kitchen wearing her blue striped morning dress that hangs loose from a yoke. It makes her eyes look even bluer and hides her condition.

"Happy birthday, Sophie," she said, sitting down on the bench beside the door. "I can scarcely believe you are already thirteen. Almost a young woman." She sighed. "That means I must be getting old!"

I did not know what to say. She does look weary.

She pushed herself up and gazed in the looking glass, smoothing her hair. "Living in the wilderness has taken its toll, I fear." She turned to me. "How I wish we were back in Dresden with its concerts and theaters and art museums."

I looked away. It sounds lovely. Someday I will go there to see for myself. Still, this is home. It is true we have no theater, but before the war people would gather in one home or another to play music and sing. Mama always loved those parties. Maybe once the war is over, she will be happy here. I was so absorbed in thought that it startled me when she spoke again.

"You are surely your father's daughter when you look like that. What are you thinking about?"

"*Ach* . . . only that Papa needs help with the milking." A lie, of course, but my thoughts belong to me.

I got an apron from the kitchen and went out the front door to pick a rose for my hair, a pink one. Mama's flower garden is blooming because Rosina and I carry water to it every day. I just hope rain comes soon or else our corn will be stunted. Then what will we do?

Papa had our four *Milch* cows in the pen beside the barn. He was tying Ophelia's calf to a fence post when I opened the gate. "Ah, what a pretty birthday *Mädchen* you are."

I said *danke* and got a stool so that I could milk Ophelia. She is as white as *Milch* itself except for her face, which is reddish brown. I sat down, leaned my head into her warm side, and started milking. The chickens clucked and pecked at the grain Papa had scattered.

"For one day, let's forget the war, shall we?" Papa said.

"I'll try, Papa."

"I have a special present to give you after breakfast." He meant my portrait. Still, it would be a surprise, because I had not seen the finished painting.

Later, as we sat around the kitchen table, Papa brought a bundle wrapped in Mama's silk shawl and set it on a chair facing me. "And now for the unveiling . . . or unshawling!" he said with a wave of his arm.

"Off! Off!" Willie cried. "I want to see."

Carefully Papa removed the shawl. My hands flew to my cheeks. It was in an oval wooden frame and glazed, making it a real portrait. Willie ran, put his finger on the glass, and said, "Sophie!"

Papa laughed. "Willie, you are the best critic in the world."

Willie looked up at him. "What is that?"

"A critic is someone who knows what he likes." Papa turned to me. "And you, Sophie?"

"You are a master, Papa." I hugged him and knelt down to study the portrait. "I love the way my eyes are looking directly out of the painting at whoever is there."

"That's what you do best, Sophie," he said.

"You are surely a master, Friedrich," Mama said. Her eyes softened as she gazed at him from her chair. "My father could see that at least."

Papa strode to her, took her hand, and bent to

kiss it. "Elisabet, will you sit for me to paint your portrait?"

"Of course I will, Friedrich—afterward." She meant after the baby is born. "Perhaps we will fall in love again."

"Just like the first time," Papa said and gave her hand another kiss, this one even longer.

Mama had told me about that first time. When she was nineteen her father hired an artist to paint a family portrait. He posed in a military costume with his wife, three sons, and one daughter. And behind his back that artist, my papa, and that daughter, my mama, fell in love.

Now they were both remembering. All at once Willie jumped out of his chair, ran to Mama, grabbed her other hand in both of his, and gave it a loud smack. We all laughed.

Rosina came soon after breakfast, bringing me a handkerchief she had embroidered. I was surprised that she could do such delicate work with her big, rough hands.

Since Mama's time is near we did not plan a party, but Papa said we could have a picnic on Cypress Creek. He would take his easel and paint, and I could invite Etta.

When it was nearly noon, Papa, Willie, and I started out. Mama and Rosina stayed on the gallery, watching us go. The cypress trees were leafed out, and in spite of the drought, purple thistle and spiderwort bloomed.

At the cypress cathedral we dismounted in a grassy place. While Papa began setting up his easel, I spread a quilt and set the picnic basket on it. Soon I heard Etta call my name from the crossing downstream.

"We're here!" I answered.

Willie plopped down beside the picnic basket and peered inside. "I'm hungry."

"As soon as Etta gets here, we'll eat," I said.

When she arrived, everything started to move faster. She jumped down from her horse, untied her bonnet, and jerked it off. "Mama made me wear this bonnet, but I hate it. She might as well make me carry a parasol!" She sashayed about, pretending to hold one over her head. Then she caught hold of my hands and we danced around in a circle until I was dizzy and we both collapsed on the quilt beside Willie.

"I'm hungry," he said.

Etta did not seem to hear. "Thirteen!" she said, breathlessly. "But we'll never grow up, will we, Sophie?"

I said nothing, but I knew that was not possible. Especially in times of war.

"Can we eat now?" Willie asked.

Papa chuckled and came to join us. "Can you think of nothing but your stomach, *Männlein*?"

He shook his head. "*Nein.*"

After lunch Etta and I took Willie down to the water's edge while Papa began to sketch. We sat on the cypress roots that curl like huge snakes on the bank before dipping down into the creek. Etta and I dangled our bare feet in the water, but Willie's legs were too short. So we held him by the arms and dipped his feet in the water. How he did kick and squeal! Then he climbed into my lap, and I dried his feet with a towel.

Suddenly, the horses whinnied. I turned and caught my breath. Upstream, some twenty feet away, the same Indian I had seen before sat on his red horse.

Etta pointed, screaming, "Indian!"

Willie started crying, and I clutched him close to me.

Papa faced him with only his brush in hand. "*Alemán.*"

"Papa," I whispered, "he's the same one."

"Penateka," he said, holding up two fingers together.

Papa made the same sign. For a moment no one moved or spoke. I noticed that he had something in his other hand. A small but thick black book!

"*Hermosa,*" he said, motioning toward the easel.

Papa nodded. "That means beautiful." He knows Spanish from his trips to San Antonio.

The Indian dismounted. "*Jefe* Tsena."

"Chief Tsena," Papa told us. Pointing to himself, he said, "Friedrich."

Tsena glanced at Pegasus and spoke in Spanish.

Papa turned to me. "You are right, Sophie. He says he saw the girl and white horse before."

"*Como Caballo Espíritu,*" Tsena went on.

"Like Spirit Horse, the famous white stallion of the plains," Papa interpreted.

Tsena pointed to himself and shook his head. "*Pero no tomo.*"

"But I do not take." Papa said. Then he tore off the top sheet of paper, raised his brush, and motioned the chief to come closer. "*Pinto* . . . I paint."

The chief nodded and moved to a nearby rock. He assumed a pose, one foot on the rock with the book clutched to his bare chest. Papa took out a pencil and began to draw.

I looked at Etta. Her mouth hung open. It was the first time I had ever seen her speechless. I pointed to Papa and, with Willie in my arms, we climbed the bank. Willie hid his face against my shoulder.

"It's all right," I told him. "He's friendly."

We sat down on the blanket to watch. I longed

62

to know more about the chief. Where did he come from? What was that book?

When Papa finished a quick sketch, he took up his brush and began to add color. Willie became so bold that he ran to Papa and stood holding his trouser leg. Papa dabbed a little red paint on Willie's nose, which made him squeal and made Chief Tsena grin. I wondered if he had a young son too.

Papa painted the chief's lean brown face and body, his silver breastplate, his black braids, the red and blue designs on his leggings and breechcloth, and the book in his hand with its gold-edged pages.

Then he stood back to have a look. "So, it is finished." He tore off the sheet and offered it to the chief.

Tsena took the painting in hand and studied it. Slowly a smile came over his face. "*Me gusto mucho.*"

"He likes it very much," Papa said.

Tsena held out the black book. "*Para usted.*"

"For me?" Papa took it and looked at the title in gold letters. "*The Iliad?*"

I could scarcely believe it.

The chief nodded. "*Sí*, Ill–ee–ahd." He went on in Spanish, but I could not understand.

"Very old words about a war like now," Papa translated. Then he asked where the book came from.

"Linnville."

That was a town on the Gulf Coast that the Comanches attacked and burned years ago. Tsena would have been only a boy then. How odd that he chose to bring back a book.

Papa opened the book. "*Puede leer?* Can you read?"

Tsena spoke many words I could not understand, much less remember. When he finished, Papa explained.

"He learned to read from a white boy who saved his life. The boy's father was a doctor in San Antonio. When Tsena was only sixteen years old he was held prisoner in San José Mission, but he escaped. The doctor and his family hid him in their house."

There was a pause, and suddenly I had an idea. "Papa, we have food left. Let's invite Chief Tsena to eat with us."

"*Gut* idea, Sophie. Spread it out on the blanket and fetch some water."

Etta took the pitcher to the creek while I got out the food. Then Papa motioned toward the blanket and asked Tsena to take food with us.

Tsena smiled and came to sit on the blanket. He nodded to each of us.

I cut the cake and handed it around. For a time we ate silently. Then Tsena spoke a lot of Spanish words to Papa.

When he stopped, Papa said, "*Verdad!* Truly!"

He turned to me. "He smoked the peace pipe with *El Sol Colorado*, The Red Sun. That's what they call Meusebach, the man who made a treaty with them."

"Penateka ... *alemanes* ... *amigos por siempre*," Tsena said.

"*Sí*," said Papa. "Friends forever."

Tsena unfolded his legs and stood. He thanked us and said goodbye. Then he spoke some words that I shall never forget. "*Algún día correspondo a el favor*."

It means "Someday I return the favor."

Tsena rolled the painting and stuck it in his bowcase. Then he turned, leaped on his horse, and galloped off along the creek to the north.

"Did that really happen?" asked Etta.

Papa chuckled. "*Ja*, amazing the power of painting. I have never met an enemy when I'm at my easel."

"The food helped too," I said, and everyone laughed. "But how can I ever write all this in my journal? Will you teach me some Spanish, Papa?"

"Of course I will." Then he handed *The Iliad* to me. "Happy birthday, Sophie. I am sure it is one you will never forget."

True, but for one lovely day I *had* forgotten the war.

Thursday, May 1
May Day

At school this morning the boys went down to the creek and cut a young cypress for our Maypole dance. They stripped all but the upper branches. Meanwhile we girls wove flowers into a wreath for the top. Then we fastened long ribbons of all colors to the trunk.

As usual *Herr* Steves assigned Thomas to dig a hole for setting the Maypole. He loves to show off his muscles for the girls. Christine, of course, is the May Queen, and Eduard is her king. I have to admit, they are a handsome couple.

By noon all was ready, and our parents began to arrive with picnic baskets. Mama could not come, but Papa brought Willie with him on Bucephalus. Mama had made a wreath of pink roses, and Willie held it out to me like a crown.

"*Danke*, Willie." I kissed him and placed the wreath on my head. "How is that?"

Willie nodded eagerly.

I was wearing my white muslin that *Grossmutter* sent before the war. It has a pattern of pink roses on the borders of the tiered skirt. Rosina added a ruffle of plain white around the bottom since I am taller now, if not fuller.

Etta and I took our places in the circle around the Maypole and picked up our ribbons. Eduard stood beside the Maypole, tall and straight, awaiting his queen. He wore a cape thrown over one shoulder and a crown of mountain laurel.

Suddenly, Christine swept between Etta and me in her satin cape and crown of red roses. Her elbow jabbed me on the arm. She tossed her blonde curls over her shoulder and glanced back. "Oh, excuse me, *kleine* Sophie."

How dare she call me that! Just because she is growing breasts and I am still a child. Only Papa can call me *kleine*.

"She thinks she's Helen of Troy," Etta whispered. "I should have tripped her."

"I wish you had." I could not bear the smug expression on Christine's face and looked at Eduard instead. He was looking at me with a smile. Had he heard what Christine said? Was he laughing at me?

Just then *Herr* Schimmelpfennig took up his violin and commenced playing. We danced around the Maypole, weaving in and out, raising and lowering our ribbons. The music took hold of my body, and I forgot about all else, even Eduard.

When the Maypole was wrapped with ribbons,

Willie ran up, took my hand, and started pulling me over to Papa. "Come on, Sophie. Time for the picnic."

As we passed by Eduard, he said, "You should have been the May Queen."

Ach! Did he really mean it? Before I could think, Willie had pulled me over to Papa.

"Dancing around the Maypole becomes you, Sophie. You are positively glowing," Papa said.

At that moment Thomas Boyd's father stepped up to Papa. "That's a mighty pretty daughter you have there, Guenther." I think *purty* is the way he pronounced it.

Papa thanked him, took my arm, and started to move away.

"I saw your cartoon in the newspaper . . . the one about General Johnston," he went on. "Sure wouldn't be good for you if the Vigilance Committee saw it."

All my lovely thoughts fell to the ground and shattered like the glass strawberry.

Papa's grip tightened. He stopped and turned to Mister Boyd. "I don't fear ruffians."

Mister Boyd glared at him. "You're making a big mistake, Guenther," he said and stalked off.

It filled me with dread. "Is he one of them, Papa?"

"I don't know, Sophie, but don't worry."

I could not help worrying, and if truth be told, I think Papa was worried too. More and more I feel as if we are on an island in a sea of rebel rabble.

Saturday, May 3

No sooner had I opened my journal tonight than
Max began to bark. Horses were coming up the
road from Cypress Creek. I stood and looked out
the window. A group of mounted men stopped at
our gate. *Gott im Himmel!* It was the Vigilance
Committee!

Max barked and lunged at the gate. If anyone
dismounted and tried to enter, he would attack. He
is fearless, but he could not handle a half dozen
armed men.

I flung on my robe and ran through Papa's studio
and down the stairs to the landing. Moonlight shone
through the window behind me. I watched Papa take
down his rifle from above the door. It is always
loaded and ready to fire.

"The horn, Papa!"

"Go back upstairs, Sophie."

I pretended to start upstairs, but I had no inten-
tion of doing so. Silently I crept down and saw Papa
unlock the door and go out on the gallery. I ran to
the doorway.

"Max, come," Papa said.

Max stopped barking and came to Papa.

"Who is it then?" Papa demanded. "What do you want?"

"The Vigilance Committee," came the answer. "We're looking for traitors."

My heart jumped and started pounding. I did not recognize the voice, but Mister Boyd could be out there.

"Get off my land," Papa said, "before I blow you off."

I heard rustling behind me. Mama stood there, one hand on the piano to support herself, the other on her stomach.

"Get off, I tell you!" Papa raised his rifle.

"*Nein*, Papa!" I whispered.

"I wouldn't use that if I was you, Guenther."

Papa did not move. I wanted to run out and pull him inside and lock the door.

"We don't like your way of thinking, Guenther. Either you join the Confederates or you'll hang from that tree yonder."

For once—blessed once—Papa kept his silence.

"You think real hard about it now, you hear? We'll be back for an answer." He jerked his horse around, and the men started off at a gallop.

Papa stood watching them go. As the sound of the galloping horses faded away, he lowered his rifle.

Suddenly, Mama moaned. I turned just in time to see her sag against the piano and hug her body.

"Elisabet!" Papa cried, leaning his rifle against the

wall. He caught her as her knees began to fold, carried her into their room, and laid her on the bed.

"The doctor, Friedrich," she moaned.

Just then Willie called from his room. Papa and I looked at each other. "I'll go to Willie," I said.

"*Ja*, tell him Mama is sick and you have to take care of her while I go for Doctor Pfeiffer." He cupped his hand around Mama's cheek. "I'm going, Elisabet. Sophie is here."

Mama nodded. "Hurry then."

Papa hung the rifle in its place and motioned me out to the gallery. "Lock the door and make a fire in the stove, Sophie. Put on a big kettle of water." He looked closely at me there in the moonlight. "Most of all, stay with her and assure her that Doctor Pfeiffer is on his way. Hold her hand when the pains come."

I nodded, and Papa hurried off toward the barn.

"Ma-ma!" Willie called again.

I went to him, closing the door between their rooms.

He was sitting up in bed. "*Nein*, I want Mama!"

I took him in my arms while he fought me. "Willie . . . Willie, it's all right. Mama can't come just now. She is not feeling well, and Papa has gone for Doctor Pfeiffer." I rocked with him, and gradually he stopped struggling.

"Be Mama's *Männlein* and go back to sleep,"

I crooned. "Mama will be better tomorrow, but you must stay in bed. Do you promise?" I felt him nod his head against my chest. "*Guter* boy," I said and laid him down.

I tiptoed into the kitchen and closed the door. My hand trembled as I opened the fire box and uncovered the coals with a stick of kindling. What if the baby comes before Doctor Pfeiffer does?

When I had water heating on the stove, I hurried back to Mama's room with a fidibus and lighted the candle beside her bed. She turned to look at me. Even in distress she was beautiful with her blonde hair spread over the pillow.

"You know nothing of having a baby, Sophie," she whispered.

"*Nein*, but Doctor Pfeiffer is on his way."

"I know." She turned away and gathered the bedclothes into her fists. In a moment she began to moan and turn her head from side to side. "Sophie, help me."

"What, Mama? What shall I do?" Then I remembered Papa's words: *Hold her hand.* I took her hand in mine, and she held on. The clock struck midnight. I listened for hoof beats. "*Lieber Gott*, let Papa come soon," I whispered. It is funny how you can wonder what *Gott* is, but when trouble comes, you pray.

Mama began to squeeze my hand tighter and

tighter. She arched her head back and screamed. I was afraid the baby might be coming.

"Mama, tell me what to do."

"Sophie!" Willie cried from his room.

She released my hand. "Go, Sophie."

Willie lay in his bed, whimpering. "I'm sad . . . for . . . Mama," he said in jerky little gasps. "Is she . . . going to . . . die?"

"*Nein*, Willie, *nein*. Her stomach hurts, but she won't die. I promise. You can help her by trying to sleep." I pulled him onto my lap and began to sing the lullaby that Mama always sings.

"Sleep, Willie, sleep.
Your papa is watching the sheep . . ."

His little body grew limp in my arms, and his breathing became slower, deeper. Now and again I heard Mama moan. I knew she needed me to hold on to, so I laid Willie on his bed and pulled the bedclothes up to his chin.

"Mama's *Männlein*," I whispered.

"All right, Sophie."

When I returned to Mama, she reached out her hand. I sat down beside her and held it. As I watched her face, I heard the horses coming. A blessed sound!

"I hear them, Mama . . . Papa and Doctor Pfeiffer. I'll go let them in."

She smiled and seemed to sink into the bed.

I waited at the door to make sure it was really Papa. Then I heard Max's happy yelps and unlocked the door.

"How is she?" Papa asked.

"It hurts her, Papa, but the baby hasn't come yet."

"*Gut*," said Doctor Pfeiffer. His cheery face and pink cheeks made me feel better at once. "You may bring the kettle now, Sophie, and some towels."

After I had done so, he closed the door to Mama's room. I lighted the lamp on the dining table and sat down with Papa.

"Why don't you go up to bed, Sophie?"

"It's all right, Papa. I want to wait with you."

He smiled. "Very well."

"Papa, those men . . ." I started.

"Not now," he said, shaking his head.

I nodded. Still, I could not put them out of my mind. Would they return?

We sat, waiting. Whenever Mama cried out, Papa leaped up and walked about.

After a time Willie called, "Sophie?"

I went to him, and he raised his little arms. I picked him up and carried him into the living room. "Mama is going to be all right, Willie. Doctor Pfeiffer is here." I sat in the rocker, and Willie looked over at Papa to see if that was really true. Papa nodded and smiled at him.

I began rocking. "I'll sing you a song if you close your eyes." Sweet Willie closed his eyes, and I sang softly.

"You, you live in my heart dear,
You, you live in my mind . . ."

He snuggled up to me. Maybe it was the song or the beating of my heart that soothed him—or both. He soon fell asleep. I rested my head on the back of the rocker and closed my eyes. The next thing I heard was a tiny cry.

Papa was up, standing at the closed door. In a moment it opened, and Doctor Pfeiffer said, "Come, Friedrich, and see your fine baby daughter!"

Papa motioned me to come also. With Willie asleep on my shoulder I followed him. Beside Mama lay a little bundle. Only her head was visible, and it had lots of thick black hair!

Papa leaned over and kissed Mama. "Elisabet! Another beautiful daughter."

Mama looked pale and weak, but she smiled. "*Ja, mein Lieber.* May Magdelene Elisabet Guenther."

"How about Lena for short?" Papa said.

Mama nodded. "I want to take her back to Germany, Friedrich."

Papa hesitated a moment. "We'll talk about it when you are stronger, *Liebchen*. I promise."

Mama's words made me remember the Vigilance Committee, and for the first time I wanted to leave Texas too. But I knew, and Papa knew, that was not possible.

Now it is after midnight. Tree frogs are warbling their lullaby from the creek, but I could not sleep until I wrote everything down.

Friday, May 9

Those men have not returned, but Chief Tsena did.

When I got home from school today he was talking to Papa at our side gate with Willie standing between them. Fortunately Mama has to keep to her childbed for a few more days, or she would have made Papa send the chief away.

Willie ran to me. "Sophie, Chief Tsena brought pemmican." He held up a slice to show me and put it in his mouth. "It's good."

I dismounted and Willie took my hand, pulling me to the gate. I nodded to Chief Tsena. "*Buenos días.*"

He nodded in return. "*Buenos días.*"

"The chief tells me his band is moving farther west to the Nueces River," Papa said. "He came to say farewell."

"Oh, that's too bad. I could have taught him to read some more English words."

Papa chuckled and told Tsena what I had said.

He looked at me and smiled. "*Gracias, señorita.*"

Then I had a thought. "Papa, I could teach him some words now, couldn't I? As a farewell gift?"

"Sure, you could do that. Go find a book and

we'll sit on the gallery." He opened the gate for me and motioned Chief Tsena to enter. "Oh, and Sophie, tell Mama that it is all right."

I went straight to Papa's desk, opened the glass doors of the bookshelf, and got the big Shakespeare book. On the way out I stuck my head into Mama's room. Baby Lena was asleep in her cradle, so I whispered. "Chief Tsena is here, and I'm going to read some words to him."

Mama raised her head and opened her mouth.

"Papa said to tell you it is all right. Don't worry."

She closed her eyes and let her head fall back on the pillow.

Papa and Chief Tsena were sitting side by side at the edge of the gallery. Willie was drawing on the swept path with a stick—painting, he calls it. I sat down next to Papa and opened the book.

"Sophie, those words are too hard and the print too small for someone just learning. Why don't you just read aloud?"

"But he won't understand, Papa."

"That's all right. The words sound good anyway." He turned to Chief Tsena. "Sophie *leyó* Shakespeare." He pronounced the name carefully.

"*Och!*" the chief said. "*Yo sé* Shakespeare."

"He knows Shakespeare, Sophie!"

"*Verdad?*" I asked.

78

Tsena nodded. He spoke in Spanish to Papa, and seemed to make a request.

I looked at Papa.

"He wants you to read the last words of *All's Well that Ends Well*," he said.

Willie came and sat beside me and I read:

"All yet seems well, and, if it end so meet,
The bitter past, more welcome is the sweet."

"What does that mean?" Willie asked.

I put my arm around his shoulders. "It means, if the past is bitter, more welcome is the sweet." I turned to Papa. "Can you explain that in Spanish?"

"I'll try." He thought a moment and turned to speak to Tsena.

The chief smiled and nodded. "Shakespeare *habla la verdad*." Papa said that meant Shakespeare speaks the truth.

Then Tsena stood. "*Ahora adiós*." Now farewell.

"*Momento*," Papa said. "Sophie, go get a loaf of bread that Rosina baked this morning."

"*Ja*, Papa." I hurried to the kitchen, wrapped one in a towel, and brought it to Chief Tsena.

"*Muchas gracias*." He turned and walked to the gate. "*Hasta luego*." Until then.

"*Hasta luego*," Papa and I said.

"Asta go," said Willie, waving as the chief mounted his red horse.

I watched him ride away, wondering if there would ever be a *luego*, a then.

Saturday, May 10

The war goes on. Union forces have won some victories along the Mississippi River. At the end of April they attacked New Orleans from the Gulf and now occupy it—again at a great loss of lives on both sides. It is madness.

Here at home Lena turned one week old today. This morning I took her out on the gallery and sat down in the rocker. As I held her in the crook of my arm she stared at me with her blue eyes. Mama's eyes.

"*Guten Morgen*, Lena," I said. "I'm Sophie."

She blinked. After a time of rocking she closed her eyes and slept, her warm little body limp in my arms.

I could see Papa, Willie, and Arlis, our hired man, working on the rock fence between the road and our cornfield. Arlis was breaking rock. Willie brought small pieces to Papa for filling the cracks between the larger ones.

Beyond Papa and Willie a blue haze hung over the distant hills. The sky was white with heat clouds. It cannot rain, seemingly, and the corn will not bear unless it does. I could hear the stalks in the breeze saying, *please, please.*

Sunday, May 11

Mama let me go to another meeting of the
Comfort Militia this afternoon. When Papa and I
entered the schoolhouse, a group of men standing
near the door greeted us.

"Ah, the new father!" said *Herr* Altgelt. "Congratu-
lations, Friedrich." He turned to me with a little bow.
"*Fräulein* Sophie, are you enjoying your little sister?"

"*Ja, mein Herr.*" I nodded and went to join *Tante*
Emma. She sat alone, like a queen, smiling at me.

"I am pleased to see you here, Sophie. I trust
your mother and Lena are doing well."

"*Ja*, with Rosina's help."

"*Gut.* And what about you? Are you still keeping
your journal?"

"*Ja*, but not every day. Only when I have something significant to write."

She leaned closer. "Allow me a word of advice
from one writer to another." She put her hand
around her mouth and whispered in my ear. "Don't
let men distract you from your course. You must
write even if they want you to bear their children
instead."

I felt blood rush to my face. Without thinking,

I glanced around and saw Eduard on the other side of the room. He was looking at me, and something inside me dissolved. Is that what *Tante* Emma means? I think it is. So, here in my journal I resolve not to be dissolved by anyone.

Just then *Herr* Heuermann tapped his pipe on the table, and the men stopped talking. I noticed that the Boyds had not come today.

"You all know what happened out at Friedrich's place last week," *Herr* Heuermann began. "These ruffians come in numbers, so we must meet them with numbers." He leaned forward. "I mean no disrespect, Friedrich, but you should have sounded the alarm. We need each other if we are to protect our families."

There were murmurs of agreement, and *Herr* Altgelt stood.

"Remember, *meinen Freunden*, we are in the midst of the Confederacy. We are surrounded by those who believe in the South's way of life. Indeed, I agree with them." He let his gaze sweep around the room, taking his time.

"But we are reasonable, educated men. These ruffians are neither. They don't understand that there can be two sides to a question, and that it can be debated. *Nein*, they must fight it out. So, for this reason, we must avoid confrontation." He glanced at his wife, and I wondered if this was her idea.

83

"What do you mean exactly?" Papa asked, standing.

"I mean," *Herr* Altgelt said as he turned to face Papa, "that instead of going to war with these ruffians, we avoid them. In other words, go into hiding."

"And leave our wives and children vulnerable?" Papa shook his head. "Never!"

"Friedrich, *mein lieber Freund*, listen to me, please. What has happened to others who have met threats with violence? Tell me—you have seen it."

Papa did not answer, but his jaw clenched.

"I will remind you then. Those men have been strung up from the nearest tree, their homes burned, and their families forced to flee."

Papa looked down at the floor.

"Why is it not better to be unavailable when they come to call? Why not have a plan of escape?"

"And what of our families, Ernst?" Papa asked, looking up. "You aren't threatened. How can you understand?"

"I can imagine, Friedrich. But I believe there is less risk this way than if you threaten them. It is you they want—not your wife and children."

Papa said nothing, but I could see that he was considering *Herr* Altgelt's idea. Although it made sense to me, the thought of facing those men without Papa sent a shiver through my body.

Herr Heuermann proposed that Altgelt's plan be followed. If that did not work or if one's hiding place was discovered, then the plan was to blow the horn. He looked around. "All agreed say *ja*, all opposed, *nein*."

I did not hear a single *nein*.

Then they discussed the new conscription law.

"All the men who want to fight have joined already," said *Herr* Steves. "The rest of us, for one reason or another, feel we cannot fight."

"I for one am not blessed with good health," said *Herr* Altgelt. "Others, I am sure, have different reasons."

"*Ja*," said *Herr* Steves. "I would never take up arms against my new fatherland. Our own former governor, Sam Houston, said that plotting the destruction of the government is treason. So who are these men who call us traitors? It is they who are the traitors!"

I looked at Eduard and he at me. In the midst of the silence that followed I nodded, agreeing with our teacher. Eduard smiled and nodded back.

When the meeting was over, I went outside while Papa talked with some other men. Eduard came out too.

"I surely hope those ruffians won't come around again."

I was touched by his concern. "*Danke*, it's just that I don't know what Papa will do. I want him to be like William Tell, but I don't want him to die. And to tell the truth, I'm afraid to face them alone if he goes into hiding."

"You won't be alone. Just remember to blow the horn, and we'll come galloping to save you."

I smiled, thinking it would almost be worth the scare. "I'll remember."

Papa strode up and mounted Bucephalus. "Time to go, Sophie."

We bade Eduard *guten Abend*, good evening. My head was full of his words as we rode along Broadway to the creek crossing. There we found *Herr* Altgelt waiting for us.

"Friedrich, I want to make things right with you."

"They are right, Ernst. As right as they can be, considering we think differently."

"*Sehr gut.*" Then lowering his voice, *Herr* Altgelt said, "I want to offer my smokehouse as a refuge if you ever need it. The latch will always be open."

"*Danke*, Ernst."

On the way home Papa and I did not talk. My heart was breaking for him because he seemed broken. It was a strange feeling. Papa had finally agreed not to stand up for his beliefs. But instead of being relieved, I felt only confusion. This was not my papa,

I realized. Would I have him run for his life or stand up for it?

Shadows were creeping down the hill below our house. As we brought our horses into the barn and began to unsaddle them, Papa turned to me.

"Sophie, it's not that I feel any less sure that the Union must be saved. It's ... how shall I say it?"

I looked down. It was too painful to watch him falter.

Then he went on. "It's that I cannot bear the thought of you and Mama and Willie and baby Lena having to survive without me." He put his hand under my chin and tilted it up so that I had to look into his eyes. "If it were only my life, I would never run to the bushes."

He was pleading for my respect, and it brought tears to my eyes. "I know, Papa."

He dropped his arm to his side. "Yet it doesn't feel right. In this country a man should be able to stand up for his beliefs."

"Maybe a man must choose where to make his stand."

"Where else but at his own door?" he asked.

And then a thought came to me.

"Papa, why throw your life down before those ruffians? They are not worth it."

A little smile pulled at the corners of his mouth.

"Perhaps we men should listen to you women," he said. Then he climbed up to the loft and brought down an armful of alfalfa. While Peg and Bucephalus gathered in hay with their lips, Papa talked on. "If I am forced to take his offer, it is you, Sophie, who must speak to the ruffians."

"I guess I already knew that, Papa."

"You must say I've gone to San Antonio for *Herr* Faltin. If they threaten you, blow the horn and I'll return at once."

I swallowed and made myself say, "All right, Papa."

Sunday, May 18

Tonight I had to prove my words. Once again we were awakened by the sound of horses galloping up the road to our house. This time I did not stop to look out the window. I threw on my robe and ran downstairs.

Papa and Mama were at the kitchen door, holding each other. Then Papa released her. "Don't worry, Elisabet, I will be back if you need me."

"Go, go, Papa!" I whispered.

He handed me his pistol, and I stuck it in my belt. "Remember the horn, Sophie."

I nodded and stared at him, my heart racing. Then, with his rifle in hand, he opened the door and disappeared into the darkness.

Max barked and barked. Would they shoot him if he kept on? I hurried to the front door, unlocked and opened it. The night was as black as my ink pot. I stepped onto the gallery and called Max. He came immediately and sat at my side, growling low in his throat.

I took the horn down from the post and put my other hand on Max's head. He did not look up and lick my fingers as he usually does. His eyes were fastened on the shadowy men and horses outside our gate.

I thought of Willie in his bed and Lena in her cradle. I thought of Papa's words: *In times like these we all have to do what we are afraid to do.*

"What do you want?" I called.

"We have something to discuss with your papa, little missy," said the same voice as before.

I gathered in my breath. Papa was not far away—only across the creek. He and Eduard and others would come if I gave the alarm. "He's gone to San Antonio for *Herr* Faltin."

"Left rather sudden, didn't he?"

"No," I said flatly.

A whippoorwill sang from my climbing tree. Such a peaceful night song. I wished to be safe in my bed listening to it instead of there on the gallery. How can men want to kill each other when a bird sings like that?

"Do you like to hear the whippoorwill?" I asked.

The men laughed. Max stood up and began barking.

"*Nein*, Max." I pushed his hindquarters down, and he stopped. "Do you think if my father were inside he would let me stand out here alone?"

"Well, missy, these Yankee lovers have yellow bellies, so I ain't sure." He tossed a rope onto the gallery. "You tie that dog and go light a lantern. We'll have a look around."

I tucked the horn under my arm and picked up the rope. "*Guter Hund* . . . good dog, Max. Don't bark now." He struggled to keep a bark in his throat as I tied him.

In the kitchen I felt around on the table for the fidibus jar and knocked it onto the floor. Lena began to cry, but I could hear Mama soothing her. Picking up a stick, I opened the door of the cooking stove and got a flame. My hand shook as I lit the lantern.

"Sophie?"

I turned to see Willie standing in the doorway.

"Willie, you have to stay in your bed. Everything will be all right if you just stay in bed. I'll come to you in a minute. Please, *Männlein*."

He stared at me, then turned and disappeared into his room. I tiptoed out to the gallery.

The men had dismounted and stood inside the gate. One came and took the lantern from me. His face was covered with a bandana, like the others, so I could see only his dark, menacing eyes.

"Are the barn doors locked?" he asked.

"Yes." I hesitated. "The key is in a hole on the left."

He led the men across our garden, trampling the iris. At the barn he found the key, lifted the bolt, and went inside. The horses whinnied, banging against their stalls. I held my breath. *Please don't set it afire,* I thought.

After a time he came out, *dank dem Himmel.* They returned to the yard and walked around back. I knelt beside Max, stroking his fur and making him sit. He could sense my fear, I know, for he never ceased growling.

They strode through the peach trees and onto the gallery. Max got up and started barking. I gripped the horn, ready to bring it up to my mouth. My heart pounded wildly as they approached us. Max lunged at them, but the rope held him back.

"You shut that dog up or I will," said the leader.

"Max, *nein!*" I commanded. Fortunately, he stopped.

"That's better. We're going inside now, missy. Might find your papa hiding behind his wife's skirts."

I stood, frozen. Were they going to harm Mama or the babies? Should I blow the horn? Someone tell me what to do! But there was no one. I remembered what *Herr* Altgelt said: *Avoid confrontation.*

"Very well, if you must then," I said and stepped to the door. "It's all right, Mama. They just want to look around."

Only two of them went inside, but they made enough noise for all six—knocking over chairs, breaking a dish. But not a sound from Mama and the children. I could imagine her sitting on Willie's bed with Lena, holding her hands over their mouths. The whole house seemed to be holding its breath.

The two men clomped back out again. The one with the lantern stopped where I stood and set it down. "Guess we'll have to go and beat the bushes, but sooner or later we'll find him." He strode away, his spurs clinking.

Max and I watched them mount and ride off. Then, leaving him to guard, I went inside and turned the key.

Mama and I did not speak to each other as we got Willie and Lena settled. I rocked Willie and sang to him. At last, when he was ready to go to bed, I tucked him in.

"Are they coming back, Sophie?"

"*Nein*, not tonight."

"Tomorrow night?"

"I don't know, Willie, but I'll never let them hurt you."

And I truly believed it.

Monday, May 19

Sometime during the dark of night I heard Mama unlock the door for Papa, and at last I could fall asleep.

Early this morning Mama and I were making breakfast while Willie placed utensils beside the plates.

"Since when did you know how to handle a gun?" Mama asked, turning the sausage.

"Since I asked Papa to show me. Somebody besides him needed to know."

"Humph, not if he had any sense."

Willie looked from one of us to the other, so I said no more.

Papa came into the kitchen and put his arm around my shoulders. "Sophie, it took real courage to face those men. I'm proud of you."

"*Danke*, Papa. It surely helped that you were close by."

He nodded for a moment and turned to Mama. "But I'm not proud of myself, Elisabet. I can't live like this—hiding in a smokehouse."

Mama opened the fire door of the cooking stove and added a few sticks of wood. "Then you must go over to their side, Friedrich," she said in a level voice.

"I would rather die!" Papa said.

That tore my heart in two.

Mama slammed the fire door shut and swung around to face him. Her blue eyes were hard, the pupils like black pinpoints. "And very likely you will!"

There was a breathless silence. What if saying so makes it come true and Papa dies? It would be her fault.

"You are no longer a youth rioting in the streets of Dresden. You have a family, Friedrich," she said, blinking her eyes rapidly. "Either hide or lie!"

Willie ran to Mama and clutched her skirt. "No fighting!"

She looked down and put her hand on his curly head. But her words were directed at Papa. "Perhaps my parents were right when they disapproved of my marrying an artist."

Papa stared at her, seeming unable to believe what he had heard.

"*Ja*, Elisabet, you should have married someone more like your father!" He turned and stalked out the door.

I stirred the cornbread batter, scarcely aware of what I was doing.

Mama had told me that her father ruled their family like a tyrant. And she promised herself never to marry anyone like him. Now she seemed to wish she had never married Papa. Was this the last battle in our strange war? Was this the end of our family? I could not blame Papa if he never returned.

But he did. Later, he came in from the barn with the milk pail, dipped some water into the washbowl, and washed his hands. Then he sat down without a word to eat breakfast.

"Don't be mad, Papa," Willie said.

That broke the tension, and we all managed to laugh.

"*Nein*, Willie Boy, I won't." Papa glanced at Mama, but she did not look at him.

Tonight as I sit writing, a waxing gibbous moon has risen—the only joyful thing I have to record for this day.

Sunday, May 25

The Vigilance Committee has not returned, though every night I lie awake thinking this could be the night. What if they set our house on fire?

Lately I have taken to wandering about, looking at our treasures. Mama's piano brought from New Orleans. Above it Papa's oil painting of red–sailed ships in Venice. And the desk with its glass doors where he keeps his books. "Mental nourishment," he calls them. I cannot bear to think that some rebel rabble could take all this away from us.

Meanwhile, daily life goes on. Papa and Arlis sheared the sheep. Usually Papa takes the wool to San Antonio, but this year he is having Arlis do it. I think Papa is worried about the Vigilance Committee. Up in his studio he paints with a fury—a mythological scene of the underworld. It is all black and brown except for the pale figures of Orpheus playing his lyre as he leads Euridice up to the land of the living. But I know the story. Orpheus glances back to see if she is following. And that glance dooms her to stay with the dead. I have to turn my face away when I walk through Papa's studio.

Mama plays the piano every evening after supper.

Sometimes she sings. Her playing and singing are another reason Papa fell in love with her, he says. She charmed him with romantic songs. But now all her songs are sad.

Willie often sits beside her, watching her fingers or looking at her face when she sings. Last evening he said, "Mama, play a happy song."

She smiled at him. "Very well, *Liebchen.*"

As she began to play a polka, Willie got down from the bench and hopped about.

I held Lena up to see. "That's your funny little brother, Lena," I said. She watched, waved her arms about, and smiled for the first time. "Look, Lena is smiling already!"

Papa, who was reading at the table, came to us and bowed from the waist. "May I have this dance, *kleine* Lena?"

I gave her into his arms, and he danced her around the room. With his right hand he held her back and with his left he cradled her fuzzy head so that they faced each other like a real couple. She looked so tiny, hardly bigger than Papa's two hands.

Willie hopped over to me. "Let's dance too, Sophie."

Mama looked around at us and smiled as she played. A breeze brought the sweet scent of roses through the open door, and for a moment our home seemed happy again.

Friday, May 30

Seeing my thoughts written down in this journal clears my head. I understand now that unless the war ends soon, our family is going to fly apart.

Tante Emma feels the same way. One afternoon when she came to have coffee with Mama, she said, "I think it's high time for a little gaiety in Comfort. Why don't we have a dance under the Schimmel-pfennig Oak like we used to do?"

Mama agreed. "Maybe if we forget the war, it will go away."

Everyone in town liked the idea. The trouble is, instead of the war going away, it arrived—right there at the dance.

I should have suspected something, for this evening as we drove out in our wagon headed for the dance, my mockingbird was nowhere to be seen. I pushed the idea out of my mind. Nothing was going to spoil this night.

Mama wore her silk evening shawl, and I wore my white muslin with pink roses. Tables were set up, and everyone brought food: sausage, bread, honey cakes, ambrosia, and homemade wine. There was even a keg of beer that *Herr* Faltin ordered from San

Antonio. Chinese lanterns hung from the branches of the big tree. They swung to and fro in the evening breeze. And best of all, a full moon was rising.

Etta ran over to me, holding her skirts too high. Her frizzy hair was already beginning to pull loose from her braids. "Your husband is here!" she announced.

I put my finger to my lips. "Ssshhh!" But that only sent her into gales of laughter. I glanced around and saw Eduard. He did not seem to have heard. *Dank dem Himmel.*

When the time came for dancing, the men hoisted *Herr* Schimmelpfennig into a saddle strapped to a low branch. He likes to play his violin from on high, and the saddle makes a good seat. Dressed in his black coat and cravat, he seemed out of place in the tree with his legs dangling. As soon as he was comfortably settled, *Herr* Schimmelpfennig took up his violin and began to play a waltz. Couples started dancing— even Mama and Papa. I held Lena while Willie tugged at my skirts to come dance with him. But I did not want to look like a fool in front of Eduard.

My heart sank when I saw him step out with Christine. She had on a blue silk dress with a lace collar that made her look like an angel. An angel with breasts. No wonder Eduard danced with her instead of me. Probably he was only joking when he said I should have been the May Queen. Or maybe he said it because I'm shaped like a Maypole! Etta did not wait for anybody to ask her to dance. She asked Franz Kettner. Even though he is our age, Etta is a head taller. While she bounced on her toes, he watched his feet.

Then the music changed. *Herr* Schimmelpfennig struck up a polka. Mama came and took Lena from my arms.

Papa bowed to me. "May I have this dance, *Fräulein?*"

"With pleasure, *mein Herr.*"

I glanced up at *Herr* Schimmelpfennig perched in his saddle. He gave us a nod and turned his violin our way as though he was playing just for us. And how we danced! I forgot everything but the music and the colorful lanterns over my head. When it was over I felt so alive that I never wanted to stop dancing.

At that moment Eduard stepped up. "*Herr* Guenther, may I have the pleasure of dancing with your daughter?"

I stared at him, unable to speak. He is as tall as Papa but thinner. He wore a pale linen shirt with a blue cravat. His blond hair shone under the lanterns.

"How about it, Sophie?" Papa asked. "Would you care to dance with this young man?"

Then from up in the tree *Herr* Schimmelpfennig said, "*Ja*, Sophie, you dance with him once. He is a *guter* boy, and I command it. Just for you I play a nice waltz." He swayed to one side and began to play.

Eduard took my hand, put his other hand at my waist, and we danced. It was the first time he had ever touched me. He is such a gentleman, yet his hands are rough from work.

"So, Hedwig, my fair wife, I have returned," he said.

I looked at him and saw the way his mouth curls up at the corners when he is amused. Since I didn't want to giggle like a schoolgirl, I pretended to be Hedwig. "Oh, Tell, I suffered such anguish for you!"

"Forget it now, and live for joy alone!" he replied.

We both laughed as we whirled around and around. The lanterns and the moon and *Herr* Schimmelpfennig seemed to revolve over my head. Somehow it was easier to be Hedwig dancing with William Tell than Sophie dancing with Eduard.

When the music stopped, Eduard said, "You're a good dancer."

"*Danke.* So are you."

"Want to have some refreshments?" he asked.

I nodded and we walked to a table spread with platters of cakes and cookies and a pitcher of watered wine. We helped ourselves and stood watching the dancers for a time.

"What are you reading now, Sophie?"

"*The Iliad.*"

"So . . . the book the Comanche chief gave you."

"*Ja,* Chief Tsena."

"It is surely odd for a Comanche to have such a book."

"Not for Chief Tsena," I said. "He's different. A white boy saved his life and taught him to read a few words—even read Shakespeare to him. I think he yearns to learn more. Why else would he have taken a book when they raided Linnville?"

Eduard cocked his head. "Hmmm. That makes sense."

"Have you read *The Iliad?*" I asked.

"I have. My parents brought a copy from Germany."

"It's so bloody," I said. "So many warriors are killed, just for one beautiful woman."

"Who wasn't worth it," Eduard said.

I smiled to myself.

"But let's not talk about war," he went on. "Let's talk about after the war is over, whenever that may be. Do you have a dream of what you want to do?"

I took a sip of wine. I pondered whether I should tell him. He was looking at me intently, waiting, and something turned loose inside. "I dream of being a writer, maybe a novelist."

103

"I suspected as much. I know what a reader you are, and Etta told me you keep a journal."

That Etta! She cannot keep a secret. And yet I was pleased that Eduard knew.

"Yes, I'm writing it like a novel with dialogue."

"Will you write our dialogue?"

I felt myself blush. "Maybe some of it."

Eduard grinned. "Then I had better choose my words carefully."

"Please, don't worry. Just tell me about your dream."

"My dream is not to be a farmer!"

I laughed. "What then?"

Eduard glanced up at the moon shining through the branches "I want to go back to Germany and study at the university in Leipzig. And afterward to Rome and Greece to study the ancient ruins. You see, I dream of being an architect." He looked at me and smiled. "It's an extravagant dream for a farmer's son—even a Latin farmer."

For a moment I said nothing, absorbing his words, admiring his dream. "I like extravagant dreams."

Just then *Herr* Schimmelpfennig struck up a polka. This time he was joined by *Herr* Schmidt on the accordian.

"Let's dance," said Eduard.

We danced to the wild rhythm. It is a wonder that

Herr Schimmelpfennig did not throw himself out of the saddle!

Suddenly, it all stopped. The music, the dancing ended. Eduard released me, and I looked around. Close to a hundred men, mounted on horses, had gathered outside our circle. They were armed and wore black hats, each ornamented with a silver star. Their leader, the only one wearing a coat, had a scowl on his face. Who were they, and what did they want?

Herr Altgelt said, "Will you join us, gentlemen?"

The leader tossed his head back. "Ha! You damned Dutchmen and your music!"

Papa stepped out from our group. "Captain, or whatever your rank, there are ladies present."

"You, sir, keep your mouth shut! I have eyes to see. And what I see is a bunch of traitors!" He looked around at all of us. For a moment the only sounds were crickets chirping and the occasional snort of one of their horses.

"Governor Lubbock has declared martial law," he went on. "That means every one of you Dutchmen has to take an oath of allegiance to the Confederacy— or leave the state within thirty days." A smile spread across his face. "And I'm going to make sure you do one or the other."

I looked at Papa, and he must have sensed it for

he glanced at me. *Papa, please keep quiet*, I said silently.

It was *Herr* Altgelt who spoke. "You must not assume, sir, that all Germans are against the Confederacy."

The man turned in his saddle and looked directly at *Herr* Altgelt. "Oh? And who are you?"

"I am Ernst Altgelt, founder of this small village of peaceful souls. And to whom have I the honor of speaking?" This was *Tante* Emma's dashing cavalier at his best.

"Captain James M. Duff, leader of these two companies of Partisan Rangers. We're on our way to Friedericksburg to put down the rebellion."

"Rebellion?" said *Herr* Altgelt. "I do not think you will find a rebellion there."

"I'll be the judge of that, Mister Altgelt. In my book, anyone not supporting the Confederacy is in rebellion." Captain Duff removed his hat and made a sweeping gesture with it. "So good night, ladies. It would be wise if you kept your men on the right side of the war—that is, if you want to keep them. Meanwhile, since we are camping on the creek, there will be no more music and dancing tonight." He put on his hat, jerked his horse around, and his men followed him back toward Cypress Creek.

Herr Schimmelpfennig played two notes on his violin as if to say *gute Nacht*, and the party was over.

On the way home I asked Papa what martial law means.

"It means that the generals run the state instead of the governor."

"Then why would Governor Lubbock declare it?"

"He probably had no choice, Sophie."

Mama said nothing, but I sensed her anger.

Later that night I heard Mama and Papa arguing in their room. Then a door closed. When I tiptoed to the stair landing, I saw Papa making a bed for himself on the sofa. Sometimes I wish she were not my mother.

Back in my room, I sat down at my writing table. I wanted to escape into someone else's world, so I reached for *The Iliad* and opened it to the satin ribbon. Chief Tsena took good care of this book, for the ribbon is not soiled or frayed.

I commenced reading where I left off. This is a story about a war between the Greeks and Trojans that lasted ten years. *Himmel!* Is my war to last that long?

Prince Hector is bidding his wife and child farewell at the gates of Troy before a battle. His wife fears she will never see him again and pleads with him to stay within the walls. Of course, he does not. Three thousand years ago men were no different than they are today. Prince Hector says:

> "But go thou to thine house and see to thine own tasks, the loom and the distaff, and bid thine handmaidens ply their work; but for war shall men provide . . ."

Even though the language is hard to understand at first, I am used to it now. The story beguiles me. Will Hector die? Will his wife be widowed and his child orphaned?

If so, at least she did not turn her back on him.

Wednesday, June 4

Since school is out for the summer, Papa said I could go to Faltin's with him after dinner. This is the day mail comes from San Antonio, and *Herr* Faltin expected a wagon of supplies to arrive as well. Best of all, I knew that Eduard might be there.

Mama handed me her reticule. "If they have coffee beans, buy a pound. We could all use a little cheering up."

I nodded, even though I thought it would take more than coffee—it would take an end to the war. Slipping the drawstring over my wrist, I hurried out to the barn. Papa had put my sidesaddle on Pegasus already, so I did not protest.

We trotted down the road, across Cypress Creek, and along Main Street. It is an odd name for a street that has only a few houses and Faltin Mercantile, but *Herr* Altgelt has bigger plans for our village. At the store there were a number of horses already tied up in front, and men were gathered on the gallery, talking. My heart gave that little leap of pleasure, for Eduard was among them. He looked up and nodded to me, but he was intent on whatever the men were talking about.

109

We tied our horses to the fence, and Papa opened the gate for me. "You go on in, Sophie. See if we have some mail. I'll stay here on the gallery."

Etta ran out to meet me. "Sophie, guess what?" She took my hand and began to pull me toward the door. "There is coffee and hard candy too."

"I don't believe it. Is the war over?"

She laughed. "*Nein*, but you know *Herr* Faltin."

Just as we were going inside, I heard a stranger on the gallery say something that made me stop. Etta tugged at me, but I shook my head and put a finger on my lips.

"Why do you want to listen to all that stupid war talk?" she asked.

I shushed her again, and she whirled around and left. I didn't care, because what I heard the stranger say was, "The butcher of Friedrichsburg—that's what they call Duff!"

"Is it that bad then?" Papa asked.

"*Ja*," said the stranger. "General Hébert named him provost marshal of three counties including yours. He answers to no one. He and his men ride about the countryside, hanging Unionists and burning their homes."

"*Mein Gott*," I said under my breath. It was worse than I imagined. Papa looked stunned. Would this news be enough to make him change his mind or lie?

Herr Lange, Etta's father, was speaking now.
"They are worse than the Vigilance Committee,
Friedrich, because they have the law on their side.
The time may come when we will all have to take
the oath to the Confederacy."

Papa lifted his chin. "I am sure of one thing. If
Sam Houston were still governor there would be no
generals running the state."

"I wish he were still governor as much as you do,"
said *Herr* Steves. "But Old Sam was not willing to
take the oath, and look where it got him. Kicked out
of office!"

"And I respect him all the more for it," Papa said.
"He's a man true to his principles."

I knew then that Papa was never going to change
his mind or lie. No matter what happened.

"*Mein lieber Freund,*" said *Herr* Lange, "would Sam
Houston have clung to his principles if he faced
hanging?"

Papa's face looked grim. "That's a hard question,
Johann, but I think he would. He is no ordinary man
surely."

No one spoke for a time, but I could not move.

Then *Herr* Steves' brother, Heinrich, spoke up.
"There is another choice. You can go to Mexico and
stay until the war is over. Or sail for New Orleans
and join the Union army."

"That is a bold choice," said *Herr* Lange. "Not one I would make."

"Yet you were bold enough to leave Germany and come here," Heinrich Steves replied.

"True, Heinrich, but back then I had no choice. Now I do, and I will not stand on principle."

Many men would not, but my papa is no ordinary man either. Sometimes I wish he were.

In the silence that followed, *Herr* Faltin approached and handed me a letter from *Grossmutter* with our newspaper. For a moment I forgot the conversation on the gallery and stepped inside.

"How could a letter get through the blockade?" I asked.

"There are ways, Sophie." He looked at me with his kindly eyes and smiled. "Now, better get in line for coffee. It's going fast."

Although he did not say so, I knew he meant those ships that dare to slip through the blockade.

I nodded and went to stand in line.

Etta left a group of girls and hurried over. "Aren't you going to read your letter already? Who's it from?"

"My *Grossmutter* in Dresden, but it's addressed to Papa."

"If I were you I'd rip it right open. How can you stand to wait?"

112

I smiled at her and slipped the letter in Mama's reticule. "Because I am not you, Etta."

She put her hands on her hips. "Then at least tell me why you would rather listen to the men talk about war."

I did not want to discuss it in front of all those people. And Etta talks loud enough for everyone in the store to hear. I shook my head.

"Oh, I know why!" she said, looking triumphant. "His initials are E.M."

I said nothing and looked away.

"All right, Sophie, I'll keep my mouth shut." She opened a small drawstring bag. "Here, have a piece of hard candy."

I reached in, took one, and popped it in my mouth. Etta did the same and kept quiet while I purchased a pound of coffee beans. Then we walked out on the gallery. The group of men had broken up. Papa was outside the fence with our horses, talking to the stranger and Eduard.

"Who is that man?" Etta asked.

"I don't know."

As we stood watching, the man mounted and rode off down Main Street. Then Etta and I walked out to the gate.

"*Guten Tag*, Sophie, Etta," Eduard said, tipping

his hat. He smiled politely, but his thoughts seemed to be elsewhere.

"Who was that stranger?" Etta asked.

Eduard looked at Papa, who said, "Just a man from Friedrichsburg on his way to San Antonio."

There was a pause. I could tell that Papa did not want to talk about him.

"Time to go, Sophie," Papa said. "I have work to do, and Mama needs your help."

"I must get home too," Eduard said.

"Will you give me a ride, Sophie?" Etta asked.

"*Ja*, sure." I mounted Pegasus, and Etta climbed up behind.

Papa put the coffee and newspaper in his saddlebag, and we bade Eduard *auf Wiedersehen*.

After we left Etta at her house, I looked at Papa. I wanted to tell him that the talk about Captain Duff scared me. But he seemed engrossed in his thoughts, and I did not want to bother him with my fears. *Maybe the letter will cheer us both*, I thought, and took it out of Mama's reticule.

"Papa, we have a letter from *Grossmutter!*"

"That's a surprise. Why don't you read it on the way?"

I pulled off the wax seal and unfolded the paper. Inside was a tiny package. "More seeds, Papa. I wonder what she sent this time ..."

"You'll have to plant them and see," he said.
I commenced to read the letter:

Dresden, Saxony

January 1, 1862

My dear Friedrich:

I hope these lines will find all of you in good health. It has been a year since we last heard from you, and I worry about the war. Our newspapers say that the port of Galveston is blockaded, which must be the reason we have had no letters. Perhaps you will not even receive this one, but I must try.

From what I read, the fighting is in the eastern states. I hope that means you will be safe in Comfort.

Your father and I are as well as can be expected at our age. His shop continues to make the finest shoes in Dresden. Indeed, Lady Gertrude called your father to the palace to measure her children's feet. She would have none but *Herr* Guenther himself! So we prosper.

Are you painting, Friedrich? I hope so. I well remember watching you draw as a child, lying on the floor. You especially liked drawing scenes from *The Iliad* with all the muscular heroes—fair Achilles and brave Hector. I have those drawings yet.

Would that we could visit with you and

Elisabet and the children. Sophie must be a young lady now and Willie a big boy. I am sending Sophie some mystery seeds.

With kisses for all from your loving mother,

Anna Guenther

We crossed the creek and started up the road to our house. In the trees cicadas sang their raspy song that swelled and faded. Papa was watching a black hawk ride an updraft high overhead, and I wondered if he had been listening.

"I wish I could see those drawings of *The Iliad*, Papa."

He only nodded. I knew he was thinking about the stranger and Captain Duff.

"I heard the stranger call Captain Duff the butcher of Friedrichsburg," I said. "That scares me."

"Well, that's why *Herr* Vogel came here—to tell us about a meeting of the Union Loyal League. We have to do something to stop Duff." Papa looked over at me. "As you said once, Sophie, it's not enough to be afraid."

"May I go with you, Papa?"

He shook his head. "*Nein*, you must stay here with Mama and the babies. And you must not mention the meeting to anyone outside our family—especially not Etta."

"*Nein*, Papa."

Willie came running to the gate to meet us, and we said no more.

It is dark outside as I write these words by candlelight. Although Papa did not say as much, I know why I must stay here with Mama and the babies. Because I know how to fire his pistol. And I promised Willie that I would never let those men hurt him.

Saturday, June 7

The Texans are fighting to leave the Union. And what are the Germans doing? Meeting on Bear Creek to decide how to avoid fighting to leave the Union. They are all mad.

Papa left for Bear Creek at dawn today. After breakfast I sat down in the kitchen to churn. Through the back door I could see Rosina hoeing weeds in the garden. Arlis was hauling water from the creek to keep our tomatoes, cucumbers, and squash alive. I think the clouds have forgotten how to let go of rain. They drift slowly northward like great ships floating across the sky—flat and gray on the bottom but billowing up into fluffy white shapes.

While I churned, Mama mixed sour cream sauce for dinner. Baby Lena lay on a quilt on the kitchen floor, playing with her toes and watching her big brother. Willie played with his little wooden horse hitched up to a corncob wagon. The two of them can make me forget the war.

I reached down and tickled the bottom of Lena's tiny foot. "Are you ticklish, *Pummelchen?*" She pulled her foot away and grinned at me. I went back to pumping the dasher down and up as she watched.

Willie came to me. "Sophie, can I churn?"

"Sure, *Liebchen*."

He took hold of the dasher and began churning with quick, shallow strokes that excited Lena. She waved her arms and kicked, which inspired Willie to dance about until he bumped into the churn. If I had not lunged to grab it, we would have had buttermilk all over the floor.

Willie looked at me. "I didn't mean to, Sophie."

"I know, Willie." It is impossible to be angry at him.

"*Liebchen*," Mama said, smoothing back a loose strand of hair. "Why don't you set the table for dinner and let Sophie finish the churning?"

Willie took utensils from the cupboard drawer, one in each hand, and carried them through the doorway to the dining table carefully. Nevertheless, on his third trip he dropped a fork and brought it to Mama for washing.

"That means visitors are coming!" she said. "It's a sure sign."

Suddenly, she looked around at me, alarm in her eyes. We had the same thought. It could mean the kind of visitors that come in the middle of the night.

"I hope it's Papa," said Willie. "When is he coming?"

"Tomorrow," Mama told him.

"Too long." Willie looked so disappointed that I

promised I would read to him after supper if he was a *guter* boy.

His expression changed instantly and he began jumping up and down. "The Elves and the Shoemaker!" he chanted.

That evening when the supper dishes were done, Willie and I sat in the swing. I opened the book to the illustration of two elves in the shoemaker's shop. One is leaping with joy at the new clothes the shoemaker's wife made for them.

Willie pointed to him and squealed. "What a funny elf!"

"There was once a shoemaker . . ." I began.

"Just like *Grossvater*," Willie said, as he always does.

"That's right, Willie. This shoemaker worked very hard and was very honest, but still he could not earn enough to live upon."

When we came to the part where the shoemaker and his wife discover the new shoes, I said, "Good wife, good wife, see what has happened this night. Someone has stitched my leather into shoes."

"It's the elves!" Willie shouted. "The elves did it!"

Papa takes delight in how Willie and I love books. He says if the house should catch fire, what he cares most about saving—after our family—are the books. More than his paintings!

Now it is late and the house is quiet. Max sleeps on the gallery, so no one can approach without our knowing. I sit at my writing table with only the company of candlelight. My nightdress is pulled up to my knees to catch whatever air is stirring.

Just tonight I finished reading Book XXII of *The Iliad*. You must be wondering about the fate of Hector, dear reader. I am sorry to tell you that it was a terrible one—even worse than his wife imagined. Achilles slew him before the gates of Troy with his spear. Then he tied Hector behind his chariot and dragged his body back to the Greek ships. Hector's wife watched from the battlements and cried to the gods, but it did no good.

Ghastly deeds are done in war.

Sunday, June 8

This evening we were all out front waiting for
Papa to come home. Mama sat in the swing holding
Lena while Willie drew a man on the swept path. It
was Papa, he said. I watered the trumpet vine that
covers the trellis over our side gate. If only I could
water the whole cornfield. The corn is usually three
feet tall by now with several ears on every stalk. But
this year it has withered. The cows will have to go
without grain, and we will probably run out of cornmeal.

Then I heard a horse coming. I straightened up
and watched the place where the road emerges from
the trees. There came Papa, trotting along, wearing
his black hat and dark blue coat—even in such heat!

I flung open the gate and ran to meet him, with
Max at my side. Papa dismounted and opened his
arms. I threw myself into them and could feel Max's
paws on my side as he leaped about, yelping for joy.
Willie ran toward us on his short little legs.

Papa picked him up and held him close. "Want
to ride Bucephalus to the house?"

"*Ja!*" Willie squealed. "Bufus!"

Papa put him in the saddle, then waved to Mama.

"What happened at the meeting?" I asked.

He shook his head. "Later, Sophie. I don't want to talk about it now."

"Are you mad at us, Papa?" Willie asked.

"*Nein*, Willie, I'm thirsty. I just want to sit on the gallery and drink some cool water."

"I'll get it for you, Papa." I ran to the house, got the tin pitcher, and went out to the well. After drawing water, I returned to Papa. He drank a full glass without stopping and held it out for more.

"Almost as good as wine but not quite," he said.

While Papa played with Willie and Lena, Mama and I set supper on the table: cottage cheese, coleslaw, tomatoes, sausage, cornbread with butter, and the honey cake I baked especially for him.

By the time Mama put Lena to bed and we sat down at the table, it was growing dark. Light from the oil lamp shone on our faces and made the wine in our glasses sparkle like liquid rubies. It seemed as if we were a little island of light where the war could not reach us.

But after supper it did. I brought it on by asking Papa about the meeting.

He said nothing for a moment, and I could see that he was struggling to find the right words. He set his wine glass on the table. "Very well, I will tell you because you need to know—all of you. At the meeting we organized three companies. If necessary—if the Confederates try to make us join their forces—we'll fight."

There was a stunned silence.

It was Mama who shattered it. "Friedrich, you are such a child! We could forget the war if only you would resign yourself."

"I'm afraid that is no longer true, Elisabet. No one can forget the war. We are all going to have to fight on one side or the other."

"*Nein!*" said Willie. "No fighting."

"Unfortunately, Willie," Papa said, "I have only two choices: fight for the Union or fight for the Confederacy."

Willie's lower lip was beginning to pucker. I motioned for him to come sit in my lap and he did.

"Heinrich Steves said there was another choice," I said.

Papa turned on me. "I remember that, Sophie, but I could not go to Mexico to hide. I would go to join the Union forces ... and fight. President Lincoln is calling for three hundred thousand men to enlist."

Mama stood abruptly and looked at him with her hard blue eyes. "Could not, would not!" she mocked. "We had to leave Dresden because of all your could–not, would–not's. Now it's happening once again." She turned and rushed into their room. Willie climbed down from my lap and ran after her.

Papa propped his elbows on the table and put his face in his hands. What could I say to him that would help?

Finally I said, "Why are there no good choices, Papa?"

He looked up at me with sad eyes. "That is the way of war, Sophie." He put his hands on the table and pushed himself up. "Now I must try to make peace." He walked to the door of their room and stood there a moment.

"Elisabet?" he said.

No answer.

"No fighting," Papa said.

Willie came running to him and hugged his legs.

Now it is late. As I sit writing, Mama is playing a Chopin nocturne, my favorite one in E-flat. I got up, walked through Papa's studio, and crept down to the landing. Mama had taken down her hair, and Papa stood behind her as she played, his hands resting on her shoulders.

I did not know whether Papa meant no fighting in our strange war or no fighting against the Confederates. But I did know that, for the moment at least, he had made peace.

Wednesday, June 18

Mama sent me to Faltin's today for the mail. Papa and Arlis are busy in the pastures burning needles off the prickly pear cactus so our cows can eat the leaf pads.

I combed my hair with care and tied it with blue ribbons to match my dress. *Maybe Eduard will be there*, I thought.

As Pegasus and I neared the store, Eduard was coming from the opposite direction. The sight of him always makes my heart leap. I slid off Peg's bare back and tied him to the fence, lingering for a time.

"*Guten Tag*, Sophie," Eduard said as he dismounted next to me. "How is it going with you?"

"*Gut*, except that the war is coming closer."

He nodded and hesitated for a moment. "Can you keep a secret?"

"Of course."

"Your father may have told you that I joined the Union Loyal League. I went to the meeting on Bear Creek."

I shook my head. "*Nein*, he told me nothing. But why?"

"Because I'm worried about Captain Duff."

"A good reason *not* to join the League," I said. "That's why we have the militia."

"That's not enough for me. The war is bigger than Comfort, Sophie."

"Now you sound like Papa."

"*Gut* . . . I admire your father. My own father chooses to keep quiet."

"Maybe he's wiser."

"If so, then I choose to be a fool like William Tell."

I stared at him, not knowing what to think or say. I wondered: What is wise and what is foolish? Is it foolish to stand up? To speak out? Oh, I don't know. I turned and ran into the store.

Saturday, July 19

A whole month has passed since I last wrote. I have seen Eduard now and then at the store, but we have not talked about anything. Maybe I offended him. Or maybe all he can think about is the war and does not want to discuss it.

Things are not going well for Union forces in Virginia, according to the *San Antonio Zeitung.* They have been unable to take Richmond, the capital of the Confederacy. Probably because General Robert E. Lee is in command of its defense.

Here at home things are not going well either. General Hébert declared our county, Kendall, and other German counties around us to be in open rebellion against the Confederacy. He ordered Captain Duff to do whatever he sees fit to put down the rebellion! Everyone is worried.

Even now Papa and Eduard are away at an emergency meeting of the Union Loyal League. When Papa left this morning he promised he would return late tomorrow. All the signs have been good. My mockingbird was sitting on his usual branch. And while I pondered what to write in my journal tonight, the music box girl finished turning with her face to me.

I hope these signs mean they will return safely with good news for a change. But what could it be? That the war is over? I hardly think so. How men can fight in this heat is more than I can understand. The air feels like the inside of an oven. I long for a cool breeze carrying the smell of rain. It would be lovely to lie in bed at night without a care and listen to raindrops pattering on the roof.

The only good news is that *Grossmutter*'s seeds have come up. They are pinks! I planted them at the edge of the gallery, and now they are full of flowers in every shade of red.

Sunday, July 20

At suppertime Papa still had not come. Mama nursed Lena and put her to bed. Then the three of us sat down at the kitchen table to eat. It was Willie who gave voice to the dread in my heart.

"Why hasn't Papa come yet?" He searched Mama's face for an answer. "Did some soldiers shoot him?"

"*Ach,* Willie, *nein!*" Mama said. "What makes you say such a thing?"

"Because he said he would fight."

"Then he said he wouldn't. Remember?" Mama cooed, smoothing the frown on his forehead.

Later, when darkness began to fall, I lighted the oil lamp and far more candles than we needed. The little ones were asleep, and Mama sat at the piano playing a piece by Schumann called "Dreaming." I sat on the sofa reading Schiller's play *The Maid of Orleans*. Mama says I read too much for my own good. Good for what?

One of the best things about reading is that it can take you away to some other place and time. You can be someone besides yourself. At that moment I was Joan of Arc, leading the French army to victory.

You are probably surprised that I, who hate war,

would enjoy being Joan. I have to admit that there is something glorious about war—at least in reading about it. War makes heroes and villains. It makes people be their best or worst, and I intend to be my best.

When Max began barking, Mama stopped playing abruptly and turned to look at me. I knew the same question had sprung to both our minds. Was it Papa or the Vigilance Committee or Captain Duff and company?

Before I could lay my book aside and get the pistol out of the drawer, Max's bark changed to yelps of joy. It was Papa! I wanted to yelp too. Mama let out her breath. Then, strangely enough, as I unlocked the door, she went back to playing the piano.

"It's Papa!" I said.

She nodded, as if only glad it was not someone else.

I opened the door. "Papa!" All I could see was his dark form leading Bucephalus to the barn.

He raised his arm. "*Guten Abend*, Sophie."

Leaving the door open, I hurried into the kitchen to set out his supper, for it seemed Mama was not going to. Even when Papa stepped inside and stood behind her, a bag of flour slung over his shoulder, she did not stop playing. He set the bag down, leaned over, and kissed the back of her neck. Mama squealed like a girl, stood up, and they embraced.

"What have you brought me, Friedrich?" she said, eyeing the bag. "A pearl necklace?"

Though Papa smiled, he did not look happy. "Perhaps I should have, but you can't eat pearls. It's wheat flour from Fritz Tegener, with his best regards."

The three of us sat down at the table then, and Papa took a sip of wine. "I know you will both be happy to hear that the League has disbanded the three military companies."

"*Gut*, Friedrich," Mama said. "I am glad to hear it. You are getting some sense."

As Papa began spreading butter on his cornbread, he asked about the little ones. It seemed to me that something else was on his mind, but he wanted to eat supper before telling us. I was right. What he had to say fell upon us like a dissonant chord.

"I have been pondering something all the way home and have reached a decision."

"You will go over to their side?" Mama asked.

Papa hesitated. "*Nein*, Elisabet. Just hear me out." He took a deep breath. "Major Tegener has advised all Unionists who are unwilling to serve in the Confederate army to meet on Turtle Creek just beyond Caspar Real's place—August first."

We stared at him, waiting, scarcely breathing.

He leaned his elbows on the table and looked directly at Mama. "And accompany him to Mexico."

132

Mama gasped. "Surely you are not going to do that."

"I am, Elisabet. Several of us from Comfort are riding there together. Rosina can come and live in the house while I am away. Arlis, of course, will take care of the farm. It's the only choice I have."

Mama stood abruptly. "It is not! If only you had some sense, but you don't. So, just go . . . I don't care anymore." She hurried out of the kitchen and shut the door to their room.

We were silent for a time, as questions tumbled upon one another inside my head. How long will he be gone? What if the Vigilance Committee returns? Is he going to enlist in the Union army? Will he ever come back? Is Eduard going? I could not bear to ask because I did not want to hear his answers. Then a question came to me that might make him think twice about going.

"What if the Confederates find out?"

"We have the right to leave already."

"But the thirty days were over two months ago," I said.

"No one is counting days."

"I bet Captain Duff is."

"Sophie, I have made a decision."

Wednesday, July 30

Tomorrow is the dreaded day. Rosina has come to stay with us. She will sleep in Willie's room. Her presence is a comfort because she is as strong as a man.

I have held fast to the days, trying to keep them from passing. But they escaped from my hands one by one. During all this time Mama scarcely spoke to Papa. Willie and Lena sensed that something was wrong. Willie tended to cling to one or the other of us and would not play by himself. Lena fretted and cried more than usual.

Our strange war is over, it seems, and neither side won. If only Papa would stay here and paint Mama's portrait, maybe they would fall in love again.

I did my chores: milking, feeding the chickens, gathering eggs, watering the flowers. Papa spent most of his time outside with Arlis, branding the cattle and sheep and cutting the dry cornstalks for fodder. Fortunately, Arlis is too old for conscription and does not want to fight anyway. And Eduard is too young. Isn't he?

This morning I went to Faltin's for our mail,

and Eduard was there. He looked so manly in his gingham shirt, a bandana around his neck, and his trousers tucked in his boots. We said *guten Morgen* to each other. I scarcely knew what else to say. I could not talk about what was in the front of my mind—Papa leaving for Mexico. Nor could I ask him if he was going.

As I was about to mount Pegasus and ride home, Eduard came striding out the door.

"Sophie . . . wait," he called.

I caught my breath. Please, *Gott*, don't let him tell me he's going with Papa.

"I hope I didn't upset you that day talking about the war."

So that was it. I could breathe again. "*Nein*, you didn't upset me. But you made me realize that I don't know what I think."

"May I walk along with you for a way?"

I nodded, and we started down Main Street. The pleasure of walking together spread through my veins and flushed thoughts of war out of my head. I was leading Pegasus, and he kept coming up and sticking his head between us. "Peg likes you," I said.

Eduard grinned. "How about you?"

I stared at him.

"Do you like me too?" he asked.

"Of course I like you, Eduard."

"I mean, do you like me a lot?"

"Why do you want to know?"

"Because I like you a lot, Sophie . . . and I'm leaving."

My heart did not know whether to fly or fall.

"I'm leaving for Mexico tomorrow, and I wanted to say *auf Wiedersehen*."

I gasped. "You too, Eduard? Why would you go? You're only fifteen."

"Because seventeen-year-olds are being conscripted now. And Duff's men are taking anyone who looks close to that."

It is true that Eduard could pass for seventeen. I feel almost a child with him. Almost as if he is Papa. I knew there was no use in trying to change his mind.

He reached in his pocket, pulled out a folded piece of paper, and handed it to me. "For you."

I unfolded it carefully. There was a fine line drawing of the Parthenon as it must have looked once. "How beautiful, Eduard. Is it mine to keep?"

"*Ja*, a keepsake to remember me by."

"I'll put it in my journal."

ᴛʜᴇ PARTHENON: ATHENS

We walked down the sloping road to the creek crossing and stopped. It was shady and cool there under the tall cypress trees with the water rippling over the roots.

"This is where Old Man Owl lives," I said. "Do you want to see him?"

The corners of his mouth curled up. "Sure."

We crossed the creek, and I stepped off the road to the biggest cypress of all. I knelt beside one of its roots and pointed to the owl face.

"Here ... see his beak and his eyes? One is winking. Do you see it?"

"*Ja-ja*, Sophie, I see. Maybe he's winking because he knows what I'm thinking."

I stood and looked at him, waiting.

"I want to ask you a question," he said.

"What is it?"

"May I kiss you?"

Thoughts of Old Man Owl flew out of my head. No boy had ever asked to kiss me. I didn't know what to do. What if I never saw Eduard again? What if his last memory of me was that he asked to kiss me and I said *nein?*

So I said *ja* and lifted my chin ever so slightly. He took my face in his hands and leaned down. I saw the sunlight on his hair, the little scar above his eyebrow, his blue eyes.

Then I closed my eyes and held my breath. He kissed me lightly. Oh, wonder of wonders! Even after he straightened up I could still feel the tingle of his lips on mine.

"*Danke*, Sophie," he said. "I will write to you." Then he dipped his head. "*Auf Wiedersehen.*"

"*Auf Wiedersehen*, Eduard." Until we see each other again. I hoped the words were literally true.

He turned and walked swiftly up the road and disappeared. I forgot to tell him that I like him a lot too. But I think he knows, since I let him kiss me.

In return for Eduard's gift I copied out these lines from *William Tell* for Papa to give him when they leave.

Whoever looks around with open eyes
And trusts in God and his own ready strength
Can keep himself from danger and distress.

Now I will lay down my quill and get into bed,
filled with both joy and dread.

Thursday, July 31

Mama, Rosina, and the little ones are asleep downstairs. Or perhaps Mama lies awake in her empty bed. Out in the night the whippoorwill sings his lament. It sounds like *come back, come back.* But his singing will not bring Papa back. Or Eduard.

I picked up the candlestick and wandered into Papa's studio—so vacant and still. I stepped to his easel and held the light to it. He must have known I would stand here like this, for he had taken down the Orpheus painting and put in its place an unfinished self portrait. Papa looked out at me with a sadness in his eyes that I had noticed lately.

"Please come back to us," I said to his portrait.

Then I returned to my writing table, for I must record this awful day.

After breakfast Papa took his leave of Willie and Lena. "Willie, you must be the man of the family while I'm away."

Willie stood looking up at him. "When are you coming back?"

"As soon as I can, Willie. Be a brave boy and take care of your mother and sisters for me. Will you do that?"

"All right," Willie said, looking so small and solitary. Papa picked him up and held him close for a moment. But Willie began pounding Papa's back with his fists. "I don't want you to go!"

"I must, Willie."

Then he slumped against Papa's shoulder and began to cry quietly as if he knew he was powerless. Papa set him down and knelt beside the pallet where Lena lay on her back, watching the scene with big eyes.

"*Auf Wiedersehen, kleine* Lena."

She reached her arms up to Papa. He put his face on her bare tummy and gave her a noisy kiss. Mama was putting food back in the safe, but she turned at the sound. There were tears in her eyes. Papa went to her and for a moment they embraced. Then she turned away. Papa's arms fell limp at his sides, and he looked at me as if I could tell him what to do.

"I'll help you saddle Bucephalus," I said.

Papa strode into the living room and unlocked the top drawer of his desk where he keeps his two pistols. He stuck the six-shooter in his belt holster, locked the drawer, and put the key on a high shelf.

"You know where the key is if you need the other one," he said. Then he took down his rifle from above the door.

"I'll bring your saddlebags," I said.

He nodded.

I had to run to catch up as he headed out to the barn. "Mama will come around," I said.

"It will be too late," he said, looking straight ahead.

What did he mean, too late? I wondered but could not ask. When we reached the barn door, I said, "Papa, I'm going with you!"

"Don't be foolish, Sophie. Of course you are not going with me. Besides, who would take care of the family?"

"Rosina," I said flatly.

He shook his head. "You are the strong one, Sophie."

"I don't want to be the strong one. I want to be a child and I want you to stay here!" I was near tears and flung my arms about him as if I could prevent his leaving. He let me cling for a moment. Then quietly he unwrapped my arms.

"Sophie, I need you to be stronger than you have ever been. I would not leave if I didn't think you could be so."

"But why did you say it will be too late? Aren't you coming back?"

"I plan to, but in time of war nothing is certain."

I stared at him, unable to believe that my papa was not sure.

"Mama knows that, you know that," he went on. "Even Willie senses it. But only to you can I say it."

"Do you think I'm Joan of Arc?"

Papa actually smiled then. "If need be, Sophie."

I shook my head. "I don't think so, Papa. You know what happened to her."

"This is not Schiller's play, Sophie. This is our own story and we must be the best that we can. Always. It's the reason we are here."

I stood watching him saddle Bucephalus as if I had lost my senses. I felt numb. He was going, and I could do nothing about it.

I could hear horses coming up the road. "Are you going to enlist, Papa?"

"*Ja.*"

I followed him out of the barn. There they were, Eduard and the other men—for I guess Eduard is now a man. They sat on their horses, waiting. I reached in my pocket and handed Papa the folded poem. "Will you give this to Eduard?"

Papa nodded. There was such sadness in his eyes, such pain, that I put my hands over my face. He embraced me.

"I'll write when I know where they are sending me."

"Just go then, Papa." I clamped my lips together.

He stepped back, gripping me by the shoulders. "No matter what happens, Sophie, be strong. Be my brave girl. Remember, *fortis fortuna adiuvat.* Fortune favors the brave."

I hugged my arms against my waist and nodded, looking at him through blurry eyes.

He smiled. Then he turned and led Bucephalus to the gate. He said something to the men and handed the poem to Eduard. Through the blur I saw him tip his hat to me. I wiped the tears away and watched them ride off, behind our house and over the hill.

It seems to me that fortune does not favor the brave. It slays them. Think of Joan, of Hector, even mighty Achilles. All brave, all slain. All but William Tell.

Wednesday, August 6

Last night I was lying in bed trying to make my body relax. As soon as I convinced my arms, my legs were tense again, or my jaws. For good reason.

All at once Max began barking and rushed to the side gate. I sat bolt upright, listening. I heard the dread sound of horses galloping up the hill and saw an eerie light outside. I threw on my robe and hurried to the window.

"*Gott im Himmel!* They have torches!"

Lena was crying now. I put on my shoes, grabbed my journal, and ran downstairs. Light from the torches flickered through the lace curtains. Mama stood in the doorway of her room holding Lena. Rosina had Willie by the hand. They looked at me, but I could not think what to do. Run or stay? Either way I needed a gun, so I got the key from Papa's desk, unlocked the drawer, and took out the small pistol.

The side gate thumped against the post as Max threw himself at it, barking. I pulled the curtain aside and peeped out. The men had dismounted and gathered outside the gate, holding their torches high. If I did not go out they would set fire to the house.

145

As I started to open the door, there was a shot. Max stopped barking.

"Don't go out, Sophie!" Mama cried. "They'll shoot you too."

"Sophie, *nein!*" Willie screamed. He ran and grabbed me.

I opened the door a crack. Max lay on the ground in front of the open gate. The men stepped over him and came toward our house. With my heart pounding I locked the door and told Rosina to carry Willie.

"The back door—quick!" I whispered and handed my journal to Willie. "Hold on to this."

I flung open the door, my pistol ready, and we plunged into the night. I led the way down the path by the kitchen garden, through the back gate, and headed for the barn. Pegasus banged against the stall with his hooves and whinnied.

At the barn I stuck my finger in the chinking and found the key. Unlocking the big doors, I dashed to Peg's stall and opened it. He charged out of the barn and stopped short. The gallery was afire now. For a moment we stared. Then I saw one of the men coming around the back of the house.

"Follow me, Mama, Rosina. Run!"

We ran up the hill behind the barn with Peg trotting alongside. Mama stumbled and fell to her knees, but she held Lena safely against her shoulder. Lena, *dank dem Himmel*, made not a sound.

I stuck the pistol in my belt. "I'll carry Willie, Rosina, so you can hold on to Mama."

Rosina helped her up and we ran on through the darkness. At the top of the hill we stopped and looked back at the blazing fire. In the blind run to escape I had not given thought to what we were losing. Now it came roaring over me, even as the flames roared over our house.

"Sophie," Mama gasped, "everything . . . gone!"

I could not speak. Papa's paintings, Mama's piano, our books. It was then that I realized Willie was not holding my journal.

"Willie, where is my journal? Did you drop it?"

"Uh–oh," he said.

"Where? In the house or outside?"

"I don't know, Sophie."

"Rosina, did you see where he dropped it?"

She shook her head. "I was too scared."

My mouth opened, but I kept the words inside. *Careless little boy! All those days, all those thoughts . . . gone!*

Willie patted my shoulder. "Don't be mad, Sophie. At least Rosina didn't drop me."

Ach, what was I thinking? I kissed his cheek.

"*Nein*, Willie, I'm not mad. You are much more important than any book."

"I know," he said. "So is Max. Is he all right?"

I hesitated. "Willie . . . Max is dead."

"Will he come back?"

"*Nein*."

"Not ever?"

Something wrenched inside me. If only I could tell him that Max is in a happier place now. But I cannot. He is dead—gone. All that is left of him is in our hearts. And that is not good enough for me. Still, I said it. "You can always keep him in your heart, Willie."

He began to shake his head. That answer was not good enough for him either.

"Max is a hero," I went on, my voice thickening. "He saved our lives."

Willie put his hand on my cheek and wiped away the tears. "So did you, Sophie."

I took his little hand in mine and kissed it. For the first time I realized that it was the truth. I had saved our family. My heart swelled, for I knew Papa would be proud.

"If your father had kept quiet, this would not have happened," Mama said. "How could he be so foolish?"

I said nothing because I did not know what I thought. Was Papa foolish? Or was he brave? Or both?

"Well," Mama sighed, "we surely cannot stand here all night. We'll go to Emma's."

We made our way down to the creek. Then, with Pegasus following, we walked along the bank until we were below our house. It still blazed. After one long look I kept my eyes straight ahead, but Willie stared.

Suddenly, he pointed toward the house. "Men!" he screamed.

My heart jumped into pounding. Silhouetted against the firelight, two men rushed toward us.

"Elisabet! Sophie! Is that you?"

Mein Gott! It was *Herr* Altgelt and *Herr* Faltin.

"*Ja,*" we called.

"*Dank dem Himmel!* You are alive." *Herr* Altgelt stood, seeming not to know whether it was proper to embrace us. "We saw the fire and came as quickly as we could."

"What a terrible thing!" said *Herr* Faltin. "I was unloading supplies and saw the flames. Do you know who did it?"

"I think it was the same ones who came before," I said.

"They shot Max," Willie said. "He's dead already."

"*Ach,* Willie, *nein,*" said *Herr* Altgelt. "I'm sorry." He patted Willie's arm. "Come now, you can stay with us."

We walked across the creek and up to Main

Street. Then *Herr* Faltin went his way, and we followed *Herr* Altgelt to his house. A lamp shone in the window. As soon as he called, *Tante* opened the door and rushed out.

"*Ach*, Elisabet, you are alive!"

"And me too," said Willie.

"Especially you, Willie," *Tante* said, giving him a pat on the cheek. "Come, the smokehouse is ready. It is not exactly the Menger Hotel, but it's yours as long as you need it."

"*Danke*, Emma," Mama said. "I don't know what we shall do." Her voice wavered. "At least I have this." She pulled a small money bag from her robe pocket.

Tante Emma embraced her for a moment.

"I'll put Pegasus in the barn," *Herr* Altgelt said.

Then *Tante* picked up a lantern and led us out the back door to the smokehouse, a small, windowless log building. Inside lay five sleeping pallets with plump feather pillows. A table held a pitcher, wash bowl, towels, and soap. There was even a rocking chair in the corner. I felt a rush of gratitude.

After we got the children settled, I lay down on a pallet. Mama blew out the lantern, and darkness enveloped us. If only I could talk to her, but her mind is made up about things, and I did not want to get into an argument. Especially with Rosina there.

In my mind's eye I could see the flames burning

our house like a giant torch. Oh, if Papa knew, he would hurry home. My throat grew hard, and tears rolled out of the corners of my eyes, down my temples, and wet the pillow. I wept silently, letting them flow.

First light coming in the open door awakened me. Everyone else was still asleep. As I lay thinking about all that was lost in the fire, I began to wonder if my journal might have survived and decided to go look for it.

I slipped into my robe and tiptoed outside. Once away from the Altgelts' place I put on my shoes and hurried to the crossing. On the other side of the creek, I walked up the slope and around the curve of the road. There I stopped and stared.

Our house was a smoking ruin. The log walls were gone. The chimney stood, as did the stone walls of the *Fachwerk*. But there was no roof, and the doors and windows were gaping holes.

I started walking again as if in a dream—or a nightmare. The side gate stood open, and there I saw the body of our Max. I fell to my knees beside him. He lay as if taking a nap, but his eyes were open. The white fur under his neck was caked with blood.

"Oh, Max, you were so brave! You saved us." I stroked the black spot beside his nose that made it look crooked, and then ran my hand along his shiny black coat. He was cold and stiff. If he were alive he would lift his head and start licking my fingers.

But he was dead, and I had to bury him. I did not want Willie to see him like this. I decided to dig his grave by the gate where he died defending us. First I needed the garden spade from the tool shed, if it still existed.

I made my way through the fallen stones around the house. I could see charred pieces of furniture and fallen timbers still smoldering. They had done a thorough job. Somewhere in there were the remains of Papa's paintings, of our books, of Mama's piano.

I shook my head. "Papa, this is an awful price to pay for honor."

Outside the kitchen doorway I saw a patch of blue, like a tiny pool of water. My journal! I rushed over, picked it up, and clasped the book to my heart. Truly it was a miracle. I was meant to keep this journal!

The same day

When I returned to the Altgelts' house after burying Max, breakfast was spread on the round table in the living room. The children, four Altgelts and Willie, had just finished eating and were getting down from their chairs. *Frau* Murck, *Tante*'s mother, and Rosina were clearing their dishes away. *Tante*

Emma sent the children out to play, but Willie ran to me.

"Sophie, where did you go?"

I knelt down. "To our house. Look, I found my journal."

He gazed at it, then at me. "Did you see Max?"

"Max is buried now. I'll tell you about it later, Willie. Everything is going to be all right."

"Not for Max," Willie said.

"Willie, if you go play with Herman and George, I'll take you to see Max's grave this evening and you can decorate it."

He nodded, walked out on the gallery, and stood alone, watching the other children.

After washing my hands in the kitchen, I sat down at the table with the adults. *Tante* offered me a platter of cheese and sausage. I took some cheese. The sausage I could not face.

"Sophie," she said, helping herself to the cornbread, "I have a skirt and short gown that should fit you."

I thanked her and looked at Mama. She had on one of *Tante*'s dresses already.

"What would we do without friends like you?" Mama said and clamped her lips together.

"In times like these we Germans must help each other," said *Herr* Altgelt. "No matter which side we are on."

"How true, Ernst," said *Tante*.

"Both sides are doing terrible things," he went on. "The South in the name of state's rights and the North in the name of the Union."

Mama covered her face.

"Shall we talk of other matters, Ernst?" said *Tante*. "We women know very well what the men are fighting about. We just don't understand why."

We ate in silence. I remembered what Papa said: *Perhaps we men should listen to you women.* In this household it seems that *Herr* Altgelt does so.

When we finished breakfast, *Tante* brought me a blue and white striped skirt and a short gown of blue calico. "There are underclothes laid out on my bed for you," she said. "Hurry, now ... I want you to go to Faltin's and see if he has any coffee. Ernst says a wagon of supplies came in."

After dressing I walked along Main Street to the store. Men stood talking on the gallery.

"Sorry to hear the news, Sophie," said *Herr* Steves.

"*Ja*," *Herr* Heuermann said. "Our militia should have been on the alert."

"I should have blown the horn, but we barely had time to escape," I said.

"Was it the Vigilance Committee?" asked Doctor Pfeiffer.

154

"I think so."

"James Boyd may be part of that gang," said *Herr* Steves.

Herr Heuermann nodded. "*Ja*, I think you're right. We need to run him out of here."

"Well, he has already run," said *Herr* Vogel. "Left his wife and young children with nothing. She came to our house begging some cornmeal. Said Thomas had gone off to join the Confederates."

Doctor Pfeiffer shook his head. "These bacon farmers have the same morals as their hogs."

I was glad to hear that Thomas had left, but there was no telling where his father might be. If only we could build a wall around Comfort to keep the rebel rabble out.

The moment I entered the store, women crowded around me, saying, "Poor child" and "How is your mother?" and "Are the children all right?" and "How fortunate you were to get out alive." All well–meaning, I know. But I did not want to answer their questions and tell the story again. I just wanted to buy coffee and leave.

Then Etta burst through the door like a bolt of lightning. Her red hair seemed charged with elec-tricity. "Listen, Sophie, I'm sorry about your house. But I have a plan—and my parents agree." She paused dramatically. "You can come and live with us until your family finds something else. We'll be sisters! I've never had a sister or brother."

Of course, I knew that. The truth is I did not think I could bear her prattling for twenty–four hours a day, even though a little of it was cheery.

Perhaps she saw my misgivings, for she added, "And I promise to let you have some peace and quiet, Sophie."

I smiled because I think she really meant it.

"So you'll come then? My mother is hoping you'll make a lady out of me someday!"

"I'll ask Mama."

"*Gut!* I'll run home and get everything ready." She darted out the door.

I moved to the counter to buy coffee.

"Unfortunately, there was none in this shipment," *Herr* Faltin said. "But for you, *Fräulein*, I have some beans from my personal stores. You wait here." He strode out the back door to his house across the yard.

When he returned I tried to pay him, but he refused the money. "It's the least I can do," he said. What a dear man.

I brought the coffee beans back to the Altgelts' and found Arlis sitting in the living room, his hat in his hands. His grizzled hair was plastered to his head, and he looked uncomfortable in *Tante*'s velvet armchair.

"First thing is to round up the cows and sheep," he was telling Mama. "I'll start out early tomorrow." Then he stood and said he had work to do at home.

Mama opened her money bag and took out a gold coin. "You may be gone for a few days, Arlis, so I'll give you this."

After he left, Mama and I went out to the smokehouse. It was time for Lena's nap, and I wanted to ask her about staying with Etta. Mama changed Lena's diaper and sat down in the rocker with her.

"Mama, Etta invited me to stay at her house until we find something else. Is that all right?"

She nodded. "*Ja*, that would take some of the burden off the Altgelts." She rocked Lena for a moment. "I just cannot believe it, Sophie—everything gone! And it's all your father's fault. If only he had some sense."

I turned away from her to keep from saying what was in my heart. *If only you loved him, maybe you could have persuaded him to change his mind.*

"Why do you turn away, Sophie? What are you thinking?"

"My thoughts belong to me, Mama."

"I know you are taking your father's side, no matter how foolish he is."

I swung around to face her. "I don't want to take sides, Mama. One war is enough. I only know that Papa said in times of war there are no good choices."

Mama's eyes grew hard. "He was wrong. He could have made a good choice."

"And hate himself," I said.

She leaned forward in the rocker, and Lena awoke, crying. "Tell me, Sophie, would that be worse than this?"

"I don't know!" I screamed.

Willie came running into the smokehouse and flung himself onto Mama's knees. "No fighting, no fighting."

Mama and I both stopped and looked at him in silence.

I knelt down, opened my arms, and he came to me. "You are right, Willie. No more fighting."

Later, just before dinner, I took him by the hand. "Come, Willie, I want to talk to you." I led him out on the gallery, and we sat in the swing.

"What, Sophie? Is it *gut* or bad?"

"Neither. It's just something that must be."

He looked at me curiously with his wide blue eyes.

"I am going to stay at Etta's house for now."

"*Nein–nein–nein!*" Willie cried and wrapped his arms around me. "I don't want you to go."

"I know, but I will be just down the street. I'll

come to see you every day, I promise. Anyway, you have Herman and George to play with."

Willie said nothing, but he did not let go of me.

"You're getting to be such a big boy, Willie, that I'll tell you something Papa told me. If you sit up straight."

He sat up. "What?"

"Papa said in time of war there are no good choices."

"What does that mean?"

"It means, *Liebchen*, that no one can do exactly what he wants. But you have to do your best, no matter what happens."

He looked straight ahead and nodded. "All right, Sophie."

After the little ones had eaten, we adults—for I was more adult than child—sat down to noonday dinner. The table was spread with platters and bowls of sliced ham, green beans in cream sauce, fresh tomatoes, boiled potatoes, and sauerkraut. In a strange way it seemed like we were having a party to celebrate the burning of our house.

When our plates were served, *Tante* gave the signal to begin by picking up her knife and fork. "I'm surely sorry you are leaving us, Sophie, but I know you will enjoy being with someone of your own age."

I could not think what to say. She made me feel like I was deserting her.

159

Herr Altgelt said, "Elisabet, I shall inquire around town to see if we can find better living quarters for you and the children—at least until Friedrich returns."

Mama smiled. "*Danke*, Ernst, you are most kind." She glanced at me as if to say, *You see? There are sensible men in the world.*

In the evening Willie and I went out to the pasture near the mill to get Pegasus. I slipped on a bridle, set Willie on the horse's back, and climbed up behind him. Willie said nothing on the way. As we came up the hill to our ruin, he turned and wrapped his arms around me.

"You know what I think, Willie?"

"What?" His voice sounded muffled.

"I think when Papa comes back, we'll build a new house right here—a stone house even better than our old one."

Willie did not answer for a moment. Then he said, "But we can't bring Max back, can we?"

"You know we can't, Willie." I dismounted and helped him down. "Come now, let's look at Max's grave and see what we can find to decorate it with."

"Where is it?"

I opened the gate. "Here, where he defended us."

Willie looked at the mound of earth. "Max is under there?"

"*Ja.*" I took his hand. "Let's see what we can find."

We stepped among the fallen stones, making our way to the back of the house. Willie's room was a mess. We saw charred pieces of his bed and scraps of his quilt, all burned around the edges. I picked him up and he hid his face against my neck.

Then all of a sudden he said, "My horse! I played with him under the climbing tree. Let's look, Sophie."

I carried him around to the front of the house. "There they are!" he squealed and wiggled to get down. Between the roots stood his wooden horse and the rider with painted yellow hair. Willie ran and picked them up. "This is for Max." He strode to the side gate, knelt down, and placed the horse and rider on top of the mound.

"Oh, Willie." I felt my throat harden. "Max would like that. I can see his tail wagging."

"You can?"

"*Ja*, in my mind."

Willie thought a moment. "So can I, Sophie."

Now it is late as I sit writing in Etta's room upstairs. Everyone in the house is asleep, but I could not go to bed until I recorded all this in my journal.

Thursday, August 7

This morning Etta and I went out to pick what was left of the squash and tomatoes for her mother to preserve. I have always enjoyed picking the garden because my mind can wander freely. But these days I don't want to think.

"Doing this together is surely more fun," Etta said.

I nodded.

"I know this is not very nice," she went on. "I mean, I know the only reason you are here is because your house burned down, but I wish you could live with us all the time and we could be sisters, but I know you wish you had your house back again so you could have a room of your own and didn't have to listen to me all the time, don't you, Sophie?"

She stopped to take a breath and looked at me out of the corners of her eyes. "Don't you dare answer that question!"

I smiled.

"You'll have to admit that living with us is more peaceful than with the Altgelts."

"*Ja*," I said, and smiled again.

"All right, Sophie, I'll be quiet already."

We went on picking squash. After a time I began to think about our ruined house and Papa being gone and how nothing would ever be the same again.

"Why don't we recite poems?" I said.

Etta nodded. "All right. You go first."

Since there will be a full moon day after tomorrow, I thought of a poem by Goethe. "This is the first verse of 'To the Moon,'" I said, and recited:

> "Fill hill and vale again,
> Still, with softening light.
> Loose from the world's cold chain
> All my soul tonight."

"*Grosser Gott!*" said Etta. "I don't even understand what he's talking about."

That made me laugh. As we moved on to another squash vine, I could almost hear her mind at work.

Then she stood up. "I know one." She undid her braids and pulled her hair down in front of her face. "Remember 'Slovenly Peter'?" She lowered her voice and slowed her speech:

> "Here stands Slovenly Peter,
> He surely could be neater!
> His fingernails are long and curly,
> His teeth are anything but pearly.
> His hair has never felt a comb,

163

The bugs in there feel right at home.
Even a pig is sweeter,
Phooey, Slovenly Peter!"

I laughed until tears came to my eyes, and it
turned into crying. I covered my face. "Oh, Etta . . .
I'm afraid Papa will never come back."

Suddenly, she was kneeling beside me, her arm
around my shoulders. "He'll be back, Sophie . . . as
soon as the war is over. You'll see."

I nodded and dabbed my eyes with the corner of
my apron. She did not know for sure, but saying so
made me feel better.

This evening I had supper with the Altgelts. Then
I walked out to our place with my journal in hand.

At the side gate I hesitated. If only Max would
come bounding up, wagging his plumey tail. But
there was no sign of life—no cicadas, no mockingbird, no sheep grazing. I stepped up to the front
gallery and peered through the gaping hole that was
once our front door. The inside walls had collapsed
into a jumble of stones and charred timber and ash.
It smelled like a fireplace that had not been cleaned
out. I wondered if there was anything left that I could
save.

Gathering my skirts, I stepped through the doorway and climbed over the rubble. Sunlight came

slanting into the house from above, which made the ruined walls seem ancient and our lives inside them long past. Here Mama sat and played the piano, and on the wall above hung Papa's painting of red-sailed ships. Over there our dining table stood and there our sofa, facing the fireplace. And that pile of charred wood in the corner was the stairway to Papa's studio and my room. A hard lump came to my throat, and everything grew blurred.

I made my way through the debris to the kitchen. There, in the midst of ruin, the cookstove squatted, black and defiant. I wiped my eyes. That valiant little stove had survived the fire. It seemed almost a live thing, and I felt myself smiling at it.

Something else had survived. In the corner I saw a piece of white china sticking out of a pile of ash and broken dishes. The head and neck of the swan bowl! I took hold of the neck and slowly lifted. It was all in one piece! A survivor. I held the swan to my heart and resolved to keep it always as a good omen.

I walked around the house to the liveoaks and looked up into the branches. Though the tree closest to the house was burned, my tree survived. Leaving the swan between the roots, I climbed up and found the bottle of ink and quill in the hollow where I left them.

After writing for a time I heard horses approaching from upstream. Some twenty or thirty mounted men appeared around the bend. Confederate Rangers! Like Captain Duff's men in their black hats with silver stars.

I drew my legs up so they could not see me and watched through the foliage. They turned into the road that goes by our place, headed in the same direction that Papa's group had gone. But surely Papa and Eduard are in Mexico already. Aren't they?

Saturday, August 9

Today is Willie's fourth birthday. *Frau* Murck baked a chocolate layer cake, which he loves. I composed a poem for him and read it aloud at the dinner table.

> "Willie is a little boy,
> Who brings me happiness and joy.
> But now he's not so little anymore,
> Because our Willie just turned four."

He beamed and clapped his hands, and so did everyone else.

Later tonight, on the Langes' gallery, we waited for the full moon to rise. There was no breeze to stir the hot air. *Frau* Lange sat in the swing with her husband and smoothed back her frizzy red hair as she fanned herself. Etta and I sat on the edge of the gallery, our legs dangling. It felt as if we were on the edge of the world, waiting for something to happen. Even Etta seemed caught up in anticipation.

As the tip of the moon flashed its light at us, I held my breath. Etta's parents stopped swinging. We all watched silently until the moon rose free of the tree tops, lighting the meadow and making a silhouette of the schoolhouse.

I knew what Goethe meant. My soul felt loosened from the world.

"Now, that is surely a sight to make one forget there is a war going on," said *Herr* Lange.

I looked over at him, our village pharmacist, a man who only speaks when he has something worth saying. He felt it too.

I thought of my own papa and Eduard. Were they watching the moon rise? I wondered. And from where? Please let them be in Mexico—safe from those Confederates.

Monday, August 18

Today my soul plummeted back to earth.

It happened after supper. I walked out to our place and was about to climb up in my tree when I saw the barn door open slightly. Was it Arlis? *Nein*, he would come out to greet me. Chief Tsena? *Nein*, it was not like him to hide. Then who? An unfriendly Indian? My heart pounded. Should I run?

"Sophie," someone called. A man stepped out and motioned me to the barn.

I peered at him. It was Ernst Kramer, one of Papa's group! I flung myself toward the barn. "*Herr* Kramer! What happened? Where's my father?"

"*Ach*, Sophie, the Confederates attacked while we were camped on the West Nueces, about ninety miles from here."

Fear seized my throat with its claws, and I could scarcely draw a breath.

"Your father was wounded in the leg. I dragged him into the chaparral to hide. That's all I know."

I clamped my hands over my mouth.

"It was a surprise attack. We had no idea anyone was following us." He frowned. "Well, some people thought so . . . thought we should move on and get

169

across the Rio Grande. Your father, for one. But Major Tegener decided there was no danger, even though we left quite a trail."

I stared at his haggard face, at his dark tangled hair. I was unable to move or speak or think of anything except Papa lying wounded . . . maybe dead in the chaparral.

"The evening before the attack, we were all quite cheerful," he continued. "There was a full moon rising, and the next day we would cross the Rio Grande."

A pang shot through my heart. The same full moon I watched rising.

"We talked and sang until late in the night, completely unaware of what was to come." He looked away for a moment. "Around four in the morning a shot awoke us. Then another and another. We returned fire as best we could, but they were hidden in the cedar brakes. After that, all was quiet and we waited." He paused, seeming to gather his strength.

"Just before dawn they charged. Three times, and each time we drove them back. It was during the next charge that your father was wounded. We had used up our ammunition by then and couldn't hold our position. So we ran."

"And my father couldn't."

Herr Kramer shook his head slowly. "*Nein.*"

"But he may still be alive," I said.

"It is possible."

"What about Eduard Meyer?"

Again he shook his head. "I'm sorry, Sophie, I don't know. What I do know . . ." He closed his eyes a moment before continuing. ". . . is that they shot all the prisoners. Massacred them and left them lying there."

I gasped. Was Eduard one of them?

"One last word, Sophie. I'll be moving on tonight, but you must not tell anyone you saw me. The Confederates are searching for survivors. They have sworn to hang us all."

I shook my head, turned, and ran blindly toward the road. All I could think was that Papa had been wounded and might or might not be alive. I had to tell Mama. Yet there was nothing to do but wait.

At the creek I stopped short. Wait? For what? If Papa was wounded in the leg, he couldn't get back here or to Mexico either. He may still be lying in the chaparral. Somebody had to go find him and bring him home. The militia? No, they could never get through the Confederate patrols.

I sat down by Old Man Owl to think what to do. Then I heard a voice in my head: *But a girl might.* I looked at Old Man Owl winking at me.

"How can I ride ninety miles through the wilderness?" I said aloud.

The voice again. *How can you not?*

It was true. I couldn't leave Papa out there. If he was wounded, he needed help. If he was . . . I took a deep breath. Could I be as brave as Joan of Arc?

If need be, Sophie. Those were Papa's words.

"But how am I to know the way?"

We left quite a trail. Herr Kramer's words.

Ach, I was hearing voices like Joan. Were they from *Gott?* I had no army like Joan, but an army would be no help. I was not trying to save a country—only one man. My papa.

Ja, I have to do what I am afraid to do. I stood up and started for the Altgelts'. Surely Joan must have been afraid too, but she could not deny her voices. Neither could I. Of course, Mama would never allow me to go, so I would tell no one but Etta and swear her to secrecy.

I began to make plans. Gather supplies and leave tomorrow night. Borrow Etta's mare so I could change horses and make thirty miles a day, and have an extra horse for Papa.

By the time I arrived at the smokehouse, Mama was getting Lena diapered and ready for bed. Willie looked like an angel in a white nightshirt. I stood in the doorway, holding back the terrible news. Mama picked up Lena, and all three turned to look at me as if they expected something.

"Papa was wounded in a fight."

Willie rushed to me and grabbed my legs. "No fighting!"

Mama gasped. "How badly?"

"In the leg. That's all I know."

"Where is he?" she asked.

"Not far from the border, on the Nueces River. The Confederates followed them and attacked."

Mama lay her head on Lena's, closed her eyes, and swayed. I thought she might collapse, so I helped her into the rocker.

"Who told you this?" she said in a soft voice.

"I can't say, Mama. Just one of the men who escaped."

"Is Papa coming back?" Willie asked.

"*Ja,*" I said, cupping his face in my hands.

"How do you know?"

"I just have a feeling, Willie." It was a lie, of course.

Mama sighed. "I knew it would come to this."

Willie came and patted her shoulder. "Don't worry, Mama. Sophie knows best."

She smiled at him. "Oh, *Liebchen*, you are a sweet boy."

I held my hand out to him. "Come, Willie, time for bed. I'll sit beside your pallet until you fall asleep."

He nodded and lay down. I stroked his hair until he began drawing the deep breaths of sleep.

"I'll go to Etta's now," I whispered to Mama. "Don't give up on Papa."

She shook her head, and I could not tell whether that meant she wouldn't give up or that she had no hope.

I found the Langes sitting on the gallery.

Etta ran to me and took my hand. "Sophie, I thought you'd never come back."

"Papa has been wounded . . . There was a massacre," I heard myself say. Maybe it was the word "massacre" that brought tears to my eyes. I began to sob.

Suddenly, *Frau* Lange's arms were around me. For a long time she patted my back, murmuring, "It's all right, Sophie, it's all right."

When I pulled away at last, *Herr* Lange offered me a handkerchief. "You must not lose hope, Sophie. Your father is no ordinary man."

"That is true, *mein Herr*." I lifted my chin. "And I am his daughter." *His Joan of Arc*, I thought, thrilling with the idea. "Now, if you don't mind, I'm going upstairs."

Etta moved to follow me.

"Etta, you stay," her mother said.

Inside I lighted a candle and climbed the stairs. After undressing, I sat down with my journal and wrote all these pages. As always, it eased my mind. I know what I must do.

174

Here is a list of supplies to take:

gun	hardbread
matches	dried beef
bandage	canteen
carbolic acid	tin cup
laudanum	swan bowl for luck
wine	journal

When I got this far I heard someone climbing the stairs.

"Sophie? May I come in?" Etta asked, opening the door.

"Will you swear to keep a secret if I tell you?" I asked.

"I swear."

"I've decided to ride Pegasus out to the Nueces River to look for Papa. I'm leaving tomorrow night."

Etta clapped her hand over her mouth and stared at me. Then she said, "I'll go with you."

"*Nein*, Etta. Your parents would never forgive me."

"But what about Confederates or ... or Indians?"

"I don't know, but nothing can keep me from going. I guess I have a little of Papa's stubbornness. Anyway, I don't think the Confederates would stop a girl. I'll tell them I'm going to the Nueces to bury my father."

"But the Indians might," Etta said. "They are not

all like Chief Tsena." She stared at me as if her words could change my mind.

For the first time I remembered that Chief Tsena moved to the Nueces. Was his village near the massacre? I wish I knew.

"Listen, Etta, I need your help, not your doubts."

She bit her lips together and nodded. "What do you need?"

"Your horse, for one thing."

"*Ja*, you can take Schwarzie. What else?"

I read my list to her.

"Everything is easy but the medicines," she said. "Papa keeps his pharmacy cabinet locked and puts the key on top. We'll have to wait until they are asleep. Tomorrow night."

Tuesday, August 19

Everyone in Comfort gathered at Faltin's today, but Etta and I went about secretly gathering provisions. In the cellar we got a bottle of wine and some dried peaches. From the tin safe in the kitchen, a loaf of hardbread and a chunk of peppered beef. I borrowed her father's knickerbockers to wear under my skirts and also his canteen.

Now it is dark, and we are waiting until her parents go to bed. My plan is to ride ten miles tonight. I will follow the Guadalupe to the village of Zanzenburg and camp at the mouth of Turtle Creek. I have ridden that way before, going to Caspar Real's house, but never alone.

Here I must stop, for the clock just struck eleven. It is time for us to go downstairs and unlock the medicine cabinet. I hope *Herr* Lange does not wake up while we are at it!

Later

Etta and I started down the stairs. "Watch out for the second step from the bottom," she whispered. "It creaks."

She carried a candlestick, and I followed her. We both had on nightdresses in case we were discovered.

If that happened, Etta said, we would pretend to be getting a piece of molasses cake in the kitchen.

Once past the creaky step, we crossed the living room and peered into the pharmacy. Fortunately, the door between it and her parents' sleeping room was closed. We tiptoed over to the cabinet. Etta reached up, groped around, and found the key. I held my breath as she carefully put it in the lock and turned it. Not a sound. She opened the doors. Not a squeak.

Then she held the candlestick up so I could read the labels. The shelves were filled with bottles of all manner of tinctures and elixirs. I found the two I wanted and nodded. She closed the cabinet, locked it, and was putting the key back in place when it fell, clattering to the floor! For a moment we froze, staring at each other in the candlelight.

"Etta, is that you?" her father said from the other room.

She picked up the key, replaced it, and we fled to the kitchen. Opening a drawer, Etta took out a knife. I hid the bottles between the folds of my nightdress. We heard the door open and her father shuffle barefoot across the pharmacy. He appeared at the kitchen doorway in his nightshirt.

"What are you doing then, Etta?"

"I'm sorry we woke you, Papa. Sophie and I got hungry so I was getting a knife to cut us a piece of cake ... and it dropped. The knife, not the cake."

"Odd. It sounded like it was in the pharmacy."

"*Nein*, Papa."

He looked from one of us to the other. "Well, *gute Nacht*. You and Sophie sleep well."

As Etta uncovered the cake, we heard his door shut. I dared not look at her because, in spite of the seriousness of the situation, I knew she might start giggling. She sliced two pieces of cake and whispered, "Farewell party."

Since we have to wait until her parents go back to sleep, I opened my journal. I will end tonight by copying a letter I wrote to Mama. Etta will give it to her tomorrow.

> *Meine liebe* Mama,
>
> I have gone to look for Papa. You will surely be shocked, but there is no other choice.
>
> If Papa is wounded, I will bring him home. If he is dead, I will bury him.
>
> > Your daughter,
> > Sophie

Now it is time to go. I have changed into *Tante* Emma's short gown and skirt over the knickerbockers. Etta gave me a straw hat that ties under my chin. Papa's small pistol is tucked in my belt. The provisions are all packed in the saddle bags out in the barn. Wish me luck, dear reader.

Wednesday, August 20

On that moonless night I rode Pegasus along Main Street with Schwarzie following. Before we went down to the creek, I stopped. The crossing is a scary place in the dark. How different it seemed the day Eduard kissed me. Sunlight was sparkling on the water then.

The water was like black ink rippling over the roots and rocks. Someone could be hiding behind the trunk of one of the cypress trees. Still, if I did not have the courage to cross that creek, I might as well turn around and go back. I tugged on Schwarzie's rope and coiled it as she came up.

"Ready?" I nudged Peg with my heels. "Go!" We dashed across, splashing through the water. At the top of the bank I glanced back. "We made it, my friends."

Slowing to a walk, we continued up the hill and passed by the ruins of our house. Once it was filled with lamplight, but now it is dark and roofless. I looked away, gave Pegasus a kick, and we trotted on.

After a time I heard the sound of flowing water, the Guadalupe, and saw a line of trees silhouetted against the sky. It was still a long way to Turtle Creek, but at least I had a river to follow.

The crescent moon was rising when we passed through Zanzenburg and came to a liveoak that stands opposite the mouth of Turtle Creek. I hobbled the horses, spread a blanket, and lay down. But I dared not close my eyes. I listened for the slightest sound, perhaps a rustle of something approaching. I heard the river flowing by, the warble of tree frogs, horses cropping the grass. Nothing more.

I remembered William Tell's words: *He fears no mountains who was born among them.* I thought of the hills that surround this valley. "These are my hills," I whispered. "This is my river and my tree." The tree frogs warbled back and forth from one side of the river to the other. Many times I have fallen asleep to their lullaby. "These are my frogs." Peg's white coat shone through the darkness. I could not make out Schwarzie, but she was there. "My horses ..."

At first light I awoke to the song of a mockingbird—a good sign. I looked over at Peg and Schwarzie. "Well, we made it through the night." Peg snorted and swished his tail. Schwarzie just looked at me.

After rolling up my blanket, I untied the horses and mounted. We forded the river above the mouth of Turtle Creek where the water is shallow. On the other side we followed the creek, heading due west. I tugged on Schwarzie's rope and urged Pegasus into a trot.

The horses frisked and tossed their heads in the cool air. I looked back to the east. The sky seemed to be on fire. It reminded me of the painting Papa made of our homestead with the sun rising behind a mountain in the distance. How I hope he will make another.

We had gone some five miles when I spied the Reals' log house. It stands atop a gentle slope on the north side of the creek, shaded by a great live-oak. I could see Emma sitting on the gallery with her little brother in her lap and two other little boys play-ing at her feet. Their dog bounded to the front gate, barking.

"Someone is coming, Mama," Emma said.

"Sophie Guenther," I called, waving.

A short, plump woman came out the door—*Frau* Real. She waved back as she spoke to the dog, which looked so much like Max it made my heart ache. At the fence I dismounted.

Frau Real opened the gate and wrapped me in her arms as the children gathered around. "*Ach*, Sophie, I can't believe what has happened. We heard the news from a survivor." She released me. "What about your papa?"

"We heard that he was wounded."

"Well, we must hope for the best." She looked closely at me. "But what brings you here so early? You must have left Comfort before dawn."

"*Ja*, I'm going to look for Papa."

"*Ach, nein!* I can't let you do that. Does your mother know you are here?"

I looked at her for a moment. She is a dear lady, but she could never keep me from going. I shook my head.

"It is too dangerous, *Liebchen*. The Confederates are all around here. They won't let you through. And Indians—"

"I must go, *Frau* Real. Papa's life may depend upon it."

"*Nein*, I cannot let you take such a risk." She took my arm. "Come, let's have coffee and butterbread and talk."

I pulled away from her and began to untie Pegasus. "I have made up my mind and no one can stop me."

She looked at me with her gentle brown eyes as if to understand how I could make such a rash decision. Then she turned to Emma and the boys. "Leave us now, *liebe Kinder*, dear children. I want to talk to Sophie."

After they left, *Frau* Real said, "Did you hear about my little brother, Amie?"

"*Nein.*"

She sighed. "He was so young and hot-headed. They say that after Major Tegener was wounded, Amie shouted, 'Let's sell our lives as dearly as we can,' and led the charge." She shook her head. "But no amount of killing could ever pay for his life . . . for all their lives. He never had a chance to marry and have children. Isn't that sad, Sophie?"

"*Ja,*" I said. But even sadder, I thought, is to die and leave a family.

Then brightening, *Frau* Real said, "I've been baking bread all morning. We expect more survivors to return, and they'll be hungry. Perhaps your father will be one of them, Sophie. Why not stay with us and see? At least they will bring news."

I shook my head. "Papa was wounded in the leg, and it's not likely he could make it here."

She sighed again. "Very well, Sophie, but at least have some breakfast before you go."

Coffee and butterbread sounded good. I followed her into the house, through the front room to the fragrant kitchen. The bread was still warm and the butter sweet. While I ate, *Frau* Real wrapped a loaf for me to take along.

"Your papa and the men met in a wooded place upstream about twelve miles, near a waterhole. My Caspar says they were headed for the south fork of the Guadalupe and planned to follow it to the head-waters." She handed me the package. "You know, Anton Niess has a farm there, and I am sure his wife Bertha would welcome you."

"*Danke*, I'll stop there then."

We walked out to the gate, with the children following us. Once again *Frau* Real embraced me. "Good luck, *liebe* Sophie. Stop here on your way back."

I untied the horses and mounted Pegasus. "*Auf Wiedersehen*," I said, waving to the children.

The sun rose higher and higher as we continued along Turtle Creek. Its heat bore down on my back like a flatiron. Just beyond a deserted cabin I came upon the waterhole and decided to let the horses drink.

As I was dismounting, I heard a dry rattle. Peg shied, and I fell to the ground beside a flat rock. From the corner of my eye I saw something coil itself on top of the rock. A rattlesnake!

For one breathless moment I stared at it, absolutely still. And it stared at me, flicking its black forked tongue and shaking the tip of its upright tail.

Then I scrambled up and ran, my heart pounding in my ears. Was it following me? I gathered my skirts, stopped, and looked back. *Nein*, it was slithering off the rock into a crack underneath. I shuddered and called to the horses. When they came, I grabbed Schwarzie's rope and threw myself onto Peg's back.

Giving the snake rock a wide berth, we headed for the trail on the other side of the waterhole. It led over rocky hills and through leafy draws, and gradually my heart slowed to its regular beat.

At last we came to the south fork of the Guadalupe. Not a breath of air was stirring. The leaves drooped from the heat and drought. *Herr* Lange's knickerbockers made my legs sting. What a joy it would be to take them off and wade into the cool water. But there was no time if I wanted to get to the Niess farm before dark.

At an open place I headed Pegasus down toward the river for a drink. I looked all around. "No snakes," I told the horses as I dismounted. While they drank, I scooped up water and splashed my face. Then I took off my hat and emptied the canteen over my head.

Just then I heard a rustle and leaped up. Goose flesh prickled my skin. Was it a snake? *Nein,* only a lizard darting through dry leaves. *Ach,* what next?

As it happened, it was not snakes but men.

We followed the course of the river, heading southwest. The afternoon sun flashed through the leaves of the cypress trees that line the banks. Suddenly, Pegasus turned his ears and Schwarzie whinnied. I looked where they were looking.

Upstream on the other side, a group of mounted men were starting across the river.

"Halt!" one of them shouted.

My mind raced. If I halted they might make me turn back. But if I tried to gallop off they might shoot. I halted, and they surrounded us—a dozen men or so and pack horses.

"Good afternoon, Miss," the leader said in English. He was clean-shaven except for a mustache and wore the gray Confederate coat. "Lieutenant Williams of the Partisan Rangers. What is your name and where might you be going all alone?"

I looked straight at him. "My name is Sophie Guenther. I'm going to the Nueces River to bury my father."

"No one is allowed to go to the Nueces, Miss Guenther. Orders from Captain Duff," the lieutenant said. "You will have to turn around and go back home." He paused. "Where do you come from?"

This man could put an end to my journey, I thought, *and keep me from saving my own dear papa.* Tears brimmed in my eyes. "Comfort," I said and put my face down in my hands.

For a time the only sounds were a horse snorting, another stomping a hoof, and the rippling water of the river.

Finally, the lieutenant said, "It is no place for a

lady, Miss Guenther. You have to turn back. I'll send two of my men to escort you to Comfort. That's an order."

I wiped my eyes. *Nein*, this man was not going to stop me. "Mister Lieutenant, my father was killed. I can't bear the thought of his lying there like a dead animal."

The lieutenant looked down at the ground for a moment, then up at me. "Just how do you plan to dig a grave without a shovel?"

I shook my head. "I don't know . . . with my hands."

"Fetch the young lady a shovel," he ordered.

One of the men dismounted, took a shovel from a pack horse, and tied it to Schwarzie's saddle. Then the lieutenant motioned me to proceed. With a nod I gave Pegasus a little kick and rode off at a trot.

I could not believe my luck. He probably knew that I was hoping to find Papa alive and let me pass anyway. Not all the rebels were rabble. This one was a gentleman.

It was early evening by the time I spotted a log house on the other side of the river. Smoke rose from the chimney carrying the smell of sausage cooking. It made my mouth water. As we crossed the river and rode up the rise, dogs began to bark. A stout woman, *Frau* Niess I assumed, came out on the gallery. She waved to me and quieted the dogs.

I stopped at the gate and dismounted. Only then did I realize how sore my legs were. And I felt strangely short.

"*Guten Abend*," the woman said, opening the gate.

"*Guten Abend. Frau* Niess?"

"*Ja-ja*," she said. "You have ridden a long way?"

"From Comfort. I'm Sophie Guenther. *Frau* Real said you might have a place where I could sleep tonight."

"*Ach*, Emilie, poor thing. I heard about her brother and the massacre." She shook her head. "It is terrible indeed." Then she looked at me. "Of course you can stay, but tell me, what is a young girl like you doing out here alone?"

"I am going to the Nueces to find my father, *Frau* Niess. He was with the Unionists. We heard that he was wounded in the leg, and I just want to find him and bring him home."

"*Ach, nein!* That is too dangerous! You must have a man with you. It is my duty to stop you."

I backed away from her and clutched Peg's reins. "If I had a man with me, the Confederates would surely force us to turn around and go home." I told her about the patrol I had encountered and how the lieutenant let me pass.

"*Ja*," *Frau* Niess said, nodding, "there are gentlemen on both sides and ruffians too. I just hope you don't run into any ruffians."

189

"I have a pistol and I know how to use it."

She looked at me for a moment. "I suppose there is no stopping you, Sophie." Then she put an arm around my shoulders. "Come, you are tired and hungry. Let's see to your horses and go in the house. I have bath water heating." She took Schwarzie's rope, and we started toward the barn.

"Your father's group passed by here. It was August third, I remember, a Sunday. There must have been sixty or seventy men. And three days later the Confederates passed by. On their trail, I suppose."

If only Major Tegener had listened to Papa. With a three-day lead they could have reached Mexico before the Confederates caught up to them.

As we unsaddled the horses and rubbed them down, *Frau* Niess told me about her family, though I could hardly listen for thinking about Papa. "I'm glad for your company, Sophie. You see, my husband is off hauling supplies for the Confederates, and our two sons—only *Gott* knows where they are. They joined a frontier defense company to keep from being sent to Virginia or somewhere to fight against the Union."

How I wish Papa had done that.

We left the horses munching on mesquite hay and walked to the house. When I stepped inside, I knew I was in good hands. The whitewashed walls of the living room had blue stenciling around the windows and doors. In front of the fireplace stood an oak table with a pitcher of zinnias.

"First a proper bath," *Frau* Niess said, motioning me to follow her to the back gallery.

Together we carried the metal bathtub into her sleeping room. She brought kettles of steaming water, soap, and a towel while I carried buckets of cool water from the pump.

Then, laying a nightdress on a chair, she said, "You can wear this for supper since it will be just us girls." At the door she turned and said, "Don't forget to check yourself for ticks."

I undressed and stood in front of the mirror. Sure enough, there was a tick crawling on my stomach. Ugh! I picked it off and mashed it between my thumbnails. I found another one on my leg. Then I stepped into the tub and sat down. At first my legs stung, for they were rubbed raw. Slowly the stinging eased and I could relax. I washed myself and my underclothes with the yellow soap and sank down to my shoulders until all the soreness was gone.

Later we sat at the table spread with a white cloth. Platters and bowls of sausage, sauerkraut, green beans, sliced tomatoes, and cornbread glowed in the lamplight. I took seconds of everything, which pleased *Frau* Niess.

After supper we washed the dishes and stacked them in the cabinet. Then she brought out the Bible and laid it on the table.

"I know you Freethinkers don't read the Bible. But it's the only book I have and the only one I need." Putting on her spectacles, she leafed through the pages.

It was true. The closest thing we had to a family Bible was *The Globe Illustrated Shakespeare. Ach,* that beautiful book with its gold-edged pages—gone up in flames.

Frau Niess stopped turning pages and looked up at me. "Perhaps these words will give both of us the strength to endure whatever comes." She slid the book across the table and asked me to read the Twenty–third Psalm.

I pulled the book close and read aloud.

"The Lord is my shepherd; I shall not want. He maketh me to lie down in green pastures: he leadeth me beside the still waters. He restoreth my soul: he leadeth me in the paths of right-eousness for his name's sake. Yea, though I walk through the valley of the shadow of death, I will fear no evil: for thou art with me; thy rod and thy staff they comfort me."

"That is beautiful," I said. "I'm going to copy it into my journal tonight."

"*Ja*, the words of *Gott*." She paused. "Even though you folks don't read the Bible, I hope you believe in *Gott*."

I nodded. I did not want to discuss my beliefs with *Frau* Niess. I liked her too much, and she had already decided what she believed—or rather someone centuries ago had decided for her. Still, she makes me wonder why we Freethinkers shun the Bible. Why not read it along with all our other books?

"Time for bed, Sophie," *Frau* Niess said, standing up. "Bring the Bible and come with me." She lit a candle and led the way out back to the boys' cabin. Inside were two beds with a table and chair between them. She pointed to a small bowl on the table. "Dust yourself with that sulphur powder in the morning to keep the ticks off."

Now, after writing about this long day, I am weary. I want to believe that *Gott* is my shepherd, that he will help me find Papa alive. But I am not sure.

Friday, August 22

When I awoke, first light was coming in the windows. For a moment I lay in bed, looking around at the log and stone walls. If only this was my room at home and Papa was out in the barn waiting for me to come milk Ophelia.

But wishing would not make it so. I got up, gathered my clean underclothes from the gallery rail, and dressed.

When I stepped in the back door of the house, *Frau* Niess looked around from the fireplace. "Ah, there you are, Sophie. You'll need a big breakfast for your journey. Good food feeds the heart as well as the stomach."

How true. After breakfast my heart was filled with hope that I would find Papa alive and that Eduard had escaped.

Frau Niess and I saddled the horses, and she gave me a parcel of cooked sausage and a small pot for making broth.

"I'll pray for you, Sophie." She embraced me. "Remember, *Gott* is your shepherd."

I nodded and mounted Pegasus. "*Danke, Frau* Niess." Then I rode across the river, turned, and waved to her.

The trail continued along the Guadalupe for a way. Then it narrowed and struck out across the hills. They rose higher and steeper, becoming mountains really. There were no flat meadows between them.

At the bottom of a rocky slope, I dismounted to lighten Peg's load. The sun was at its zenith and bore down on us with all its August heat. I held the reins and started up, zigzagging, stumbling and slipping. Sweat poured from my body, taking my hope with it. I wondered how many more mountains we had to climb. Would they ever end?

After a time my legs moved on their own, and my mind began to wander. I remembered how Eduard had walked with me to the creek on that last day, how I had showed him Old Man Owl, and how he had asked to kiss me. For a moment I was there beside the purling water and felt again the tingle of his kiss.

And then I was at the top without knowing how I got there. I stood a moment to catch my breath. A hot wind swept over us, and the horses snorted, shaking their manes. After a sip of water, I tugged on the reins and we started across the top.

As we descended the other side, I heard Peg slip. Rocks came rolling past me. I let go of the reins and scrambled out of the way, but my feet slipped. I was on my back, sliding. I clawed at the rocky slope for a hold but could not stop myself until I slid into a bush and grabbed a branch. Peg kept on sliding, his forelegs stiff and his hind legs curled under him, all the way to the bottom.

I did not want to let go of the bush, even though my hands were scraped and bleeding. I stayed there watching Schwarzie slowly pick her way down with scarcely a slip. That gave me courage. Still clinging to the bush, I took one sideways step down. When that foot had a firm place, I let go and brought my other foot beside it. In this way, one step at a time, I reached the bottom.

It was an airless pit where all the sun's heat settled. I looked at my hands and pressed them to my skirt to stop the bleeding. They stung, and sweat ran down my face and body. Even though the knickerbockers were hot, they had saved my legs. I opened my canteen and poured water over my hands and patted them dry. There were no deep cuts, just scrapes. Then I tied the horses' reins and put them over their necks. We started climbing, back and forth up the mountain.

When we made it at last, I gasped. We were on top of the world! I looked across rolling hills covered with dry grass and spotted with clumps of liveoak. I felt as if I could see all the way to the Nueces.

"Papa," I called, "we're coming."

I mounted Pegasus and we headed southwest. If only the sun would not drop below the horizon. If only darkness would not come until I found him. But it would. Even though there were no green pastures or still waters here, I hoped there was a shepherd watching over me.

We moved across the high country at a trot. The horses were weary, but I urged them on. We had to find water before dark. At last the trail led us down into a ravine and along a creek. Since we had a little daylight left, I kept on. The creek emptied into a wide, shallow river. At first I thought it was the West Nueces. Then I saw the trail continuing on the other side.

"*Nein*, this must be the east fork," I told the horses.

We forded the river and picked up the trail again, heading south along the grassy bank. The sun hovered just above the horizon, and I had to find somewhere to camp. The thought of darkness falling in this wilderness filled me with dread. These were not my mountains.

As we came around a bend in the river, Peg and Schwarzie raised their heads and whinnied.

Mein Gott! At the top of the rise three Indians sat on their horses watching me. My heart lurched into pounding.

I slipped the pistol from my belt and hid it in the folds of my skirt. There were five shots—every chamber was loaded and ready to fire.

Were they Penateka? I wondered. Could they be from Chief Tsena's band? All at once I heard myself call out, "*Alemán!*"

The Indians talked among themselves. Then one turned and rode off while the other two stayed, watching me. I waited, not knowing what would happen next and afraid to move. As the sun sank below the horizon, it cast a fan of rays through the scattered clouds.

If Papa were here he would make friends with them. He would take out his easel and paint this scene: two mounted Indians silhouetted against a red sky. The magic of painting. But the only magic I had was a word—and the only defense, five shots. I clutched the gun and waited.

After a time the warrior returned with another. This fourth one started down toward me alone. He rode a red horse with golden mane and tail. I caught my breath—it was Chief Tsena! He halted a few feet away.

"*Jefe* Tsena!" I cried in a rush. "Sophie!"

He nodded.

Thoughts were clamoring to get out, but I could not speak them. All at once I had an idea—sign language. I made my left hand like a gun and pointed at my knee. *"Mi padre . . .* bang!"

He seemed to understand and motioned for me to come with him. I released the hammer carefully and slipped the pistol back in my belt.

We rode north along the river, with the other Comanches following. To think of meeting up with Chief Tsena! There must be a shepherd watching over me.

It was dark when we reached the village. Tepees glowed like lanterns beside the river. People stood watching us, and Tsena spoke to them. We stopped at the tallest tepee and dismounted as a small boy darted to the chief.

Tsena touched the boy's shoulder. "Nistiuma." Gesturing to the woman who stood beside the tepee, he said, *"Mi esposa,* Anawakeo." I knew that must be his wife. Then he nodded in my direction. "So-fee."

Anawakeo smiled and shook her long black hair over her shoulders.

Tsena pointed to the horses and then to himself. I understood that he would take care of Peg and Schwarzie. I untied Peg's saddlebags to take with me.

Anawakeo motioned for me to follow her inside, so I ducked through the opening. There, opposite the door, hung Papa's painting of the chief. I stared at it, remembering that day.

"*Por favor.*" She waved her hand toward a buffalo robe on the ground.

I sat down and looked around. Colorful designs were painted on the tepee lining. The lower edge was rolled up to catch the breeze, and a small fire burned in the firepit.

Anawakeo knelt beside me and pointed at my palms. When I showed her, she brought a small leather pouch, opened it, and sprinkled gray powder on them. Then she ducked out of the tepee, leaving me alone with Nistiuma. He watched me with his big black eyes. I smiled. He covered his face, just as Willie might have done with a stranger, and ran after his mother.

As soon as he was gone, I took the pistol from my belt, put it in the saddlebags, and got out my journal.

In a moment they returned, Anawakeo carrying a trencher of meat. "*Búfalo,*" she said.

Chief Tsena entered and sat beneath the painting. Anawakeo cut the meat, served a portion onto a stiff hide, and handed it to me. When everyone had been served, Tsena spoke some words, held up a morsel, then buried it in the firepit.

I ate with my fingers as they did. "*Búfalo muy bueno,*" I said, telling them it was very good.

Anawakeo dipped her head.

"*Su padre mi amigo por siempre,*" Tsena said. Your father my friend forever. He pointed to himself and to

me. "*Mañana vamos a* Nueces *del Oeste.*" Tomorrow
we go to the West Nueces. "*Buscamos su padre.*"
Something your father. Look for, I think.

Dank dem Himmel! No longer did I have to travel
alone. I had a Comanche chief to protect me, strange
as that may sound. Now my only worry was Papa.

After the meal Anawakeo passed around a turtle
shell of water for rinsing our fingers. Then Tsena
pointed to my journal. "*Libro,*" he said, meaning "book."

"*Sí.*" I opened it to show the handwritten pages
and picked up the pen, pretending to write.

"*Comprendo,*" he said. Then he placed his hand
beside his mouth, opening and closing his fingers.
He was asking me to read aloud.

Nistiuma said something to his mother. When she
nodded, he came and sat beside me and peered into
the book. I leafed through it until I found Saturday,
April 12. Then I pointed to the painting and began:

"Penateka ... *alemanes*... *amigos por siempre,*" Tsena said.

"*Sí,*" said Papa. "Friends forever."

Tsena unfolded his legs and stood. He thanked
us and said goodbye. Then he spoke some words
that I shall never forget. "*Algún día correspondo a
el favor.*"

Tsena was nodding. "*Sí, algún día ... mañana.*"
Yes, someday—tomorrow—he would return the favor.

Saturday, August 23

The worst and best day of my life.

Early this morning everyone in the village came to watch us leave. Chief Tsena was hitching Pegasus to a travois to carry Papa. Peg jerked his head up and shook himself to be rid of the two long poles fastened together across his withers. He turned to see the contraption behind him—a box bed mounted on the poles with an arched roof of branches.

Anawakeo was spreading buffalo robes in the box. All at once Pegasus kicked at the poles. The children laughed, and Anawakeo jumped back. Fortunately, everything was out of reach of his hooves.

I stroked his white mane. "It's all right, Peg. You'll get used to it." Gradually he calmed down.

When all was ready, I tied on my straw hat and mounted Pegasus. The poles fit neatly under my knees. As we started off, the scrape of the poles startled Peg, and he tried to bolt. But I tightened the reins and patted his neck, talking to him all the while.

We followed the river southward. Tsena rode in front, leading Schwarzie. Pretty soon the trail left the river and headed west across open country. In the distance I could see mountains. We rode toward those mountains all day as the sun rose up and started back down.

Late in the afternoon we came to the edge of a cliff and looked down at a wide river.

"Nueces *del Oeste*," Tsena said.

My heart lurched. This was the West Nueces. Buzzards circled overhead, and the cliff cast a shadow of death across the valley. I remembered the words of the Twenty–third Psalm: *I will fear no evil for thou art with me* . . .

We followed the trail along the top of the cliff and down a rubbly draw leading to the river. There we splashed through the shallow water that runs over a bed of pebbles. On the other side the bank slopes up gently to a meadow surrounded by cedar trees. The air was absolutely still. A buzzard floated down and landed among the cedar trees.

I will fear no evil, I will fear no evil . . .

Cupping my hands around my mouth I called, "Pa—pa, Pa—pa, are you here?" My voice echoed against the cliffs.

There was no answer except for water trickling over the pebbles. Maybe Papa managed to get away. Or maybe he could not hear me. I dismounted and picked up a smooth, round pebble that was golden brown with black marks and white freckles. A lucky pebble. I slipped it into my pocket.

While Tsena untied the travois and unsaddled the horses, I looked upstream where chaparral grew along the bank. Maybe that was the place *Herr* Kramer was talking about. I motioned to Tsena that I was going upstream. I took off my straw hat, got the canteen from Peg's saddle, and started out. Now and then I stopped and called Papa.

After a short distance I heard a moaning sound. I stood still and held my breath. Nothing.

"Papa?"

I heard it again—up ahead. I bolted into a run, my heart racing and my eyes searching the chaparral.

"Papa, is that you?" I called as I ran.

Suddenly, I stopped still. A dark-bearded man lay on the ground under a mesquite tree. His eyes were closed, his mouth gaped, and there was dirt or blood on his knee where his trousers had been ripped away.

"Papa!" I heard myself scream. I rushed to him, fell on my knees, and put my hand on his forehead. He was feverish, but he was alive. "*Ach*, Papa, what have they done to you?"

His eyes fluttered open and he stared at me. How could this man be my papa with his gaunt face and sunken eyes? Worst of all there was no light in them, no sign of recognition.

"Papa, don't you know me? It's Sophie. I'm here. I'm going to take you home."

His eyes rolled back in his head.

"Papa, look at me. It's Sophie."

He did not seem to hear. I looked at his leg. Through the blur I could see the oozing hole just above his knee. White things crawled around it. I wiped my eyes. Little worms ... maggots! Something rose up in my throat, and I took a deep breath. For Papa's sake I could not get sick.

I opened my canteen, got one arm under his neck, and raised him up a bit. "Papa, can you drink some water?"

I put the canteen to his lips. Without opening his eyes he took a sip, then another and another.

"*Gut*," I said and laid him back down.

At that moment Tsena rushed up and crouched beside Papa. Then, looking at me, he motioned toward the river. "*Lavamos.*"

I understood. I leaned near Papa. "We're going to carry you to the river, Papa, to wash your wound."

Tsena got his arms under Papa's arms while I grasped his ankles. We walked slowly to the river's edge. I took off his boots and socks, and we moved him closer to let the water run over his legs. Maggots began to come out of the hole, squirming and curling. I washed the blood and dirt away from the wound. The skin around it was an angry red. Then Tsena motioned me away so he could help Papa relieve himself.

Afterward we carried Papa back to our campsite and laid him on a buffalo hide with Peg's saddle for a pillow. While Tsena gathered firewood I got the wine and medicines and bandage out of my saddlebag. I mixed laudanum and wine in the swan bowl and poured it into the tin cup.

"Drink this, Papa."

He drank, and I waited for it to take effect. Then, opening the bottle of carbolic acid, I poured some into the wound. There was a lead ball in there, but I could not imagine probing for it. The carbolic acid stung my palms, but that was good. I wrapped a strip of bandage around Papa's knee. How much better to have the wound clean and covered. Of course, that did nothing for his fever. I made a wet pack with some bandage cloth and placed it across his forehead.

Tsena was laying the fire inside a circle of rocks. I got out my tin of matches and handed them to him. He seemed to know about matches. While he got the fire started, I took the cooking pot down to the river and filled it. Then I set it over the fire and added strips of dried beef.

Papa lay with his mouth open. It made my heart

ache just to look at him. I took his hand and held it in both of mine.

"Papa, you have to get well. I don't think I could live without you."

He stirred and opened his eyes. "Sophie?" he whispered.

"*Gott sei Dank. Ja*, Papa, it's me."

"Am I home?"

"Not yet, but we're going home. Chief Tsena is helping."

He closed his eyes as if he needed rest to understand.

Tsena sat nearby, watching us. When I removed the wet pack, he took it to the river for cool water. Darkness fell but the firelight kept it away. As soon as the broth was ready, I aroused Papa and got him to take a few sips. Then he turned his head aside and closed his eyes. I could only hope he would take more in the morning.

"*Su padre muy fuerte*." Chief Tsena held up his arm, flexing his muscle. "*Vive*."

"*Sí*," I said. I hoped that he was right, that Papa was strong and would live.

In a moment Tsena pointed toward the meadow above and said, "*Muchos muertos*." I knew that meant "many dead."

I gasped. What *Herr* Kramer said was true—they

had not buried the dead. The vast darkness all around us seemed to edge in closer. Please, *Gott*, don't let Eduard be one of them.

To ease my mind I got out my journal. Chief Tsena sat silently by the fire as my quill pen scratched on the paper. And gradually a sense of peace came over me. I had found Papa alive.

Sunday, August 24

Tsena kept the fire burning and I clutched the pebble all night. Once, I awoke to Papa's moans. I gave him a few sips of water and sponged his face. After a time he was quiet, so I lay down again. I closed my eyes and turned the pebble in my hand, hoping it would bring us luck.

At first light I awoke and looked at Papa. He was still breathing. Tsena was gathering wood to build up the fire. As soon as he had it going, I put the broth on to heat and got Papa to take a few sips of laudanum with wine. Then I removed his bandage. The skin around his wound still looked angry. I poured carbolic acid on it and bound up his knee again.

"Now some broth, Papa." I lifted his head and held the cup to his mouth. He opened his eyes and looked at me as if I was part of his dreaming. "Papa, it's me, Sophie. Drink now and get strong. I'm taking you home."

Later, when the travois was hitched up to Pegasus and the shovel tied to the box, we lifted Papa onto the bed of robes. Peg turned his head to watch. Then he snorted. It meant he was ready to go. We were all, horses and humans, anxious to be away from that place.

I mounted Schwarzie, and we took the first step on the long journey home. Tsena rode ahead, leading Pegasus. I followed the travois as we splashed across the river. On the other side we started up the draw. The travois bumped over the rubble, and Papa moaned.

All at once Peg slipped and went down on his hind legs. It jerked Papa's head up, but fortunately he was tied into the box bed. Tsena leaped from his horse and pulled on Peg's bridle until he got back on all fours.

At the top I rushed to Papa. His bandage was soaked with blood. I got out a length of gauze, folded it, and pressed it against his knee.

I motioned for Tsena to go very slowly, and he nodded.

At this pace we would not reach the village before nightfall. So when we came to a lone clump of liveoaks late in the afternoon, we stopped to camp. Papa's wound was still bleeding.

After I treated it and put on a fresh bandage, I saw that he was watching me.

"Sophie ... how?"

"Don't talk, Papa. I'll explain later. We're going home."

Monday, August 25

We moved slowly across the high plains, stopping often so I could give Papa sips of water. The willow roof over his bed was a lifesaver, for the sun blazed down on us.

It was dark by the time we sighted Tsena's village. The dogs started barking, but he called out and quieted them.

A few people gathered in the darkness as we stopped in front of his tepee. Tsena and another man lifted Papa out of the bed and carried him to the bushes. When they returned, we all went inside, where they laid him on a buffalo robe.

Papa opened his eyes. "Sophie ... where are we?"

"In Chief Tsena's tepee."

He just stared at me.

Anawakeo brought a bowl of tea and motioned toward Papa. I held it to his lips. He drank a little and closed his eyes. Then from outside the door someone spoke in a gritty voice.

Tsena answered, and to me he said, "Shaman."

An old man entered, nodded to everyone, and hobbled to a place beside Papa. His face was wrinkled, but his black eyes were keen. He said something to Tsena and Tsena replied, pointing to Papa's bandage.

I understood and unwrapped the bandage. The hole was oozing blood, so I pressed the gauze to it again.

"*Sangre*," the shaman said. Blood. He opened a leather pouch and took out a wad of feathery down. Waving my hand away from the wound, he pressed the down to it. "*No sangre.*"

I nodded, hoping he knew what he was doing.

The shaman leaned toward the fire and sprinkled something on the coals. It smoked and smelled like sage. He unfolded a fan and blew the smoke toward Papa while shaking a gourd and chanting. Through all this Papa lay still, his eyes closed, his face flushed.

Finally, the shaman turned to me. "*Mañana mejor.*" Tomorrow better, I think he said. He gave me the pouch of down, and I thanked him.

Tuesday, August 26

During the night I awoke, worrying whether Papa was breathing. I crawled over to him and leaned close. He took a long breath. I felt his forehead. It was cool and damp. His fever had broken!

I crawled back to my bed and lay looking up through the smoke hole. I could see one bright planet. Jupiter, perhaps. Papa would know for sure. Slowly the sky turned from black to deep blue. Day was coming, and Papa was better.

When the tepee began to fill with golden light, Anawakeo arose and kindled the fire. Then she took Nistiuma by the hand and led him outside. I sat up.

Papa and I were the only ones in the tepee. He opened his eyes and looked around. "Sophie . . . is this a dream?"

"*Nein*, Papa, it's true. We're in Chief Tsena's tepee."

"But how?"

"On my way to the Nueces River I came upon three Comanches from his village and told them I was *Alemán*."

"Surely your mother did not let you come alone."

"*Nein*, I just came. I had to, Papa. As you said, there are no good choices in war."

He nodded. Then his eyes grew intense. "Are they all right? Elisabet and the babies?"

"*Ja-ja*, Papa. Don't worry, they are fine."

I wanted to ask him about Eduard, but I dared not. That would have to wait until he was stronger.

Papa looked around the tepee until he saw his painting. "So, he kept it. I'm glad."

"*Ja*, Papa," I said, wondering how I would tell him about his other paintings.

Just then Tsena stepped through the opening. "*Mejor?*" Better?

Papa smiled. "*Sí, amigo.*"

"You must rest now, Papa," I said. "We're starting home soon."

"I . . . I'm not sure I can stay on a horse, Sophie."

"You don't have to. The chief is letting us take the travois."

"*Gracias*," Papa said and closed his eyes.

Later, Tsena and the other man carried Papa to the bushes and back again. Then Anawakeo brought in some broth. I lifted Papa's head and held the bowl to his lips.

He took a sip. "How did you find me, Sophie?"

"It was *Herr* Kramer. He managed to escape and made his way back to Comfort. He said he helped you crawl into the chaparral. That was the first word we had of what happened."

Papa seemed to drift back to that awful day. "I lay still, waiting for them to leave. And then I heard more shots. They were killing all the wounded." He closed his eyes.

"No more, Papa. You're too weak."

In a moment he opened them and went on. "Then a Confederate spied me. I thought he would kill me too. But he looked around . . . and tossed me his canteen."

"I love that man, Papa, even if he is a Confederate."

Papa nodded. "So do I."

Tsena ducked in the doorway to see if we were ready.

"*Sí*," Papa said.

Tsena, Anawakeo, and I carried Papa out to the travois. Schwarzie and Tsena's red mare stood waiting beside it. The chief was going to travel with us for a short distance.

Before mounting Schwarzie, I wanted to thank Anawakeo. I opened the saddlebag and saw the swan bowl—a dear remnant of the past. With a pang in my heart I offered it to her.

Anawakeo took the swan in both hands, holding it like a sacred object. She looked up at me and smiled. "*Gracias.*"

It was worth the loss.

As we started off, Nistiuma tried to run after us,

but Anawakeo held him back. They watched until we crossed the river and passed behind a stand of trees.

We followed the trail heading northeast, along what Papa said was Bullshead Creek. The wide valley made for easy traveling. The early morning air was cool, Papa was better, and we were on our way home. Even though we had no home, my heart sang. I had Papa with me, and that was all that mattered.

The valley soon became a narrow canyon, and the trail led sharply up to the rim. Before starting up, Tsena dismounted and checked the harnesses. Then he rode beside Papa, keeping his eyes on the travois and urging Peg on. Good Pegasus. He put his head down, watched his footing, and pulled.

When at last we reached the top, Tsena dismounted and came back to Papa.

"Amazing contraption," Papa said. "A wagon could never make it." He pointed to the travois. "*Muy bueno.*"

"*Sí, amigo.*" Tsena waved his arm toward the rolling plain, saying it was easier there. Then he said goodbye.

In Spanish, Papa thanked Tsena for saving his life.

Tsena motioned toward me. "*Su hija brava.*" Papa told me it means "your brave daughter."

"Papa, how do I say I'll never forget how you helped me?"

"*Nunca olvidó.* Never I forget."

I pointed to myself. "*Nunca olvidó.*"

Tsena nodded. He mounted his horse, raised his hand, and rode back down into the canyon.

We moved on then, and I wondered if that was the last time I would ever see Chief Tsena.

One thing was certain. He had more than returned the favor.

Wednesday, August 27

When we reached the big waterhole, I heard
horses approaching from the east—a lot of horses.
Confederates! My heart began pounding. I looked
around for a place to hide. On the south side of the
waterhole there was dense chaparral.

"Come, Peg." I took his rope, flung myself onto
Schwarzie, and gave her a jab with my heels. The
travois creaked and bounced as we trotted around
the waterhole and behind the chaparral. Some twenty
mounted men soon appeared over the rise and started
down to the water.

"*Mein Gott*, it's that Captain Duff!" I whispered.

Papa struggled to sit up.

I dismounted and went to Peg. "Good Pegasus,
you must stay quiet." I stroked his forehead as I
watched them dismount and water their horses.
What if they decided to camp here? I thought. What if
they come looking for firewood? I took out the pistol,
and held it pointed at the ground. I knew Papa was
watching me, but I kept my eyes on the men.

After they filled their canteens, a few stretched out
in the shade of some scrub oak. But Duff mounted
his horse.

"All right, you men, let's move out. We have to find us some Unionists before dark."

That sent a shudder through me. I watched as the men got up reluctantly and mounted. We stayed in hiding until the sound of their horses faded away. Since it was getting late and the way ahead was the steepest, most difficult part of the trail, we decided to camp for the night.

Friday, August 29

Two days have passed since I last wrote because I was exhausted from struggling up and down those accursed mountains. Now I sit alone at *Frau* Niess's dining table writing by lamplight. It is late and all is quiet except for the ticking of the clock and the scratching of my pen.

How pleased she was to see us. She wanted to know how I found Papa, and when I told her about Chief Tsena she said, "Well, I suppose there are good Indians too."

We helped Papa onto a bed in the boys' cabin. *Frau* Niess took off the bandage and looked at his wound. "You have done a fine job, Sophie. What we need is a bath." She brought a kettle of water, towels, and a white nightshirt and placed them on the wash-stand. "Now, *Herr* Guenther, as soon as I pour Sophie's bath I will help with yours."

While I bathed and washed our clothes as best I could with my sore hands, *Frau* Niess helped Papa. Then she prepared his supper: eggnog with brandy, buttered cornbread, and potato soup.

"You are brave to take in a Unionist, *Frau* Niess," Papa said as I gave him sips of eggnog. He had shaved, and the color in his cheeks was returning—not the flush of fever but of health. Or perhaps it was the brandy.

"It is not bravery but faith, *Herr* Guenther. Faith that *Gott* will watch over me."

"Sometimes I envy such faith," Papa said.

She smiled. "Well, I'm not educated like you people in Comfort, but I know the Bible."

"I'm sure you do," Papa said. "It is a great book of history as well as faith. But for us Freethinkers it is not the only great book." He was taking care not to offend *Frau* Niess.

She pondered a moment. "You may be right, *Herr* Guenther, but it is the only one I need."

There was a pause, and *Frau* Niess spoke again.

"One question I've always wondered about. Since you Freethinkers don't go to church, do you believe in *Gott*?"

Papa chuckled. "I can't speak for others—that is the nature of being a Freethinker. I personally believe there is a *Gott*, and I am searching for what that means."

I did not want them to get into a discussion about *Gott*, so I dipped up a spoonful of potato soup. "Here, Papa, you must eat and not talk."

"*Ja*, Sophie is right," *Frau* Niess said. "And I must see to our supper."

When Papa finished eating, I asked the question that had been on my mind—about Eduard.

"I wish I knew, Sophie. There was such confusion." He took my hand. "At least I didn't see him shot."

"Well, that is surely something."

When *Frau* Niess returned, she said, "So, *Herr* Guenther, you must get up and walk once or that leg will get stiff."

Papa sat up. Then, leaning heavily on us, he took a few steps. He winced but kept on going to the door.

"*Sehr gut,*" said *Frau* Niess. "You do that every day when you get home, now."

Home. In two more days, if all goes well, we will get back to Comfort. Sometime before that I must tell Papa we no longer have a home.

Saturday, August 30

We rode along the Guadalupe River in the shade of cypress and pecan trees. The land looked more and more like our valley, which cheered us both. Then, leaving the Guadalupe, we struck out across hills and through wooded ravines. At Turtle Creek we stopped briefly to water the horses and moved on.

Late in the afternoon I caught sight of the Real house. Their sheepdog started barking, and the whole family came out on the gallery.

"Sophie!" called *Frau* Real. She hurried to the garden gate as fast as her short legs could carry her.

The children ran to meet us and walked alongside, staring at the travois. *Herr* Real came and stood with his wife at the gate. Though not a tall man, he seems so by comparison. When we stopped, everyone gathered around Papa.

"Friedrich, *dank dem Himmel!*" *Herr* Real said.

"*Und* Sophie," Papa answered with that old light in his eyes. Then looking at *Frau* Real, his face grew serious. "I am sorry about your brother, Emilie. He was a brave young man."

She nodded. "*Ja*, too brave, I think. But you are

wounded, Friedrich. Come into the house and let me change the dressing."

As we helped Papa out of the travois, *Herr* Real said, "Where on earth did you get this contraption?"

"From a Comanche friend, Chief Tsena," I said. "The one who came to my birthday party."

Herr Real raised his eyebrows. "So," he said, nodding. "I remember that story. Remarkable."

Once we were inside, *Frau* Real brought a pan of water, towels, and medicines. While she removed the bandage, I told about meeting the Comanches on the way to the Nueces.

"You were fortunate, Sophie, very fortunate," said *Herr* Real. He stood stroking his goatee for a moment. "Friedrich, I'm afraid we can't offer you a bed, but I can show you a good place to camp for the night. The Confederates are keeping an eye on us. You must be careful. They have orders to hang all survivors and anyone who assists them."

"I know, Caspar, and I surely don't want to endanger your family."

After *Frau* Real finished treating Papa's wound, we helped him back to the travois.

Herr Real pointed behind their house toward a stand of trees in the distance. "You will be well hidden there."

"I'll send Walter with your supper," *Frau* Real said.

Now it is almost dark, and I must stop writing. Tomorrow we will arrive in Comfort. How shall I tell Papa about our house?

Sunday, August 31

At dawn Walter returned bringing coffee and bread. He showed us a back way to the Guadalupe so that we could avoid Confederates. It did no good.

We came to a wide, shallow place in the river where I decided to cross. I was looking back at the travois as the horses waded through the water when I heard a whinny.

There, on the other side, five mounted Confederates were approaching. I pulled the pistol from my belt and held it in the folds of my skirt. I noticed with a shudder that a liveoak tree stood nearby. Pegasus pulled the travois onto the embankment, and we came to a stop face to face with them. I glanced back at Papa. He was struggling to sit up.

"I'll talk to them, Papa."

The leader, a tall redheaded man, said, "Who are you, Miss, and where are you going?"

Names and answers raced about in my mind. Then I looked straight at him and lied. "My name is Henrietta Niess. My father was wounded when his gun accidentally fired, and I'm taking him to a doctor in Comfort."

"I don't believe you, Miss. I think your father was wounded at the Nueces battle."

"Oh no, sir."

He studied me a moment. "Tell me, did you ride out to the Nueces alone?"

I said nothing, just shook my head.

"Our orders are to hang all survivors."

I stared at him, paralyzed. The only sounds came from the horses, stomping their hooves, snorting.

Then a daring question came to my mind. "Do you always follow orders?"

His head jerked back. "I am a soldier, Miss."

"Are you not also a human being?" I kept my eyes on him and gripped the pistol, my thumb on the hammer. I would kill the first man who came toward Papa and the second and the third, until I could shoot no more.

He stared at me for a moment. Then he turned his horse about and talked with his men. Though I could not hear their words, there seemed to be some disagreement among them. Would they choose to hang Papa? I cocked the hammer, wrapped my finger around the trigger, and held the pistol ready to raise and fire. The sun bore down on us. The air stood still as if everything was waiting.

Finally, the redheaded man turned back to me. "All right, Miss. We have agreed that we never saw you. But be aware that your father is a dead man if Captain Duff finds out he survived." He tipped his hat and led his men off at a trot.

I uncocked the hammer, dismounted, and hurried back to the travois.

"Well spoken, Sophie," Papa said.

"You will have to stay in hiding when we get home, Papa."

"*Ja*, until my leg heals."

"And then?"

"And then I shall try once again."

My heart fell. "To go to Mexico?"

"*Ja*. What choice do I have?"

I knew he was right.

"I'll have to find another horse, but this time I'll go alone."

"Did the Confederates take Bucephalus?" I asked.

"I don't know. Probably."

By then it was noon, with only ten miles to go.

"Papa, why don't we find a shady place along the river and rest? That way it will be dark when we get home."

"*Ja, gut* idea, Sophie."

We stopped under a cypress, and I brought Papa some water from the river. It was time to tell him.

"Papa ... Mama and the children are fine, but our house is not."

He turned to me, his eyes suddenly intent. "What do you mean, Sophie? They didn't burn it, did they?"

"*Ja*, the Vigilance Committee came back."

Papa looked up at the cypress branches that spiraled overhead. He was silent for a time.

"If I had known ..." he said, taking my hand. "Tell me how it happened, Sophie."

I began, visualizing that awful night as I told the story: how Max warned us, how they shot him, and how we fled. When I finished, Papa slumped back down. I dared not tell him about the paintings. Probably he had guessed.

"I don't care about the house, Sophie. Only that you and Mama and the babies are safe. You know that." He paused for a moment. Then he lifted his head with a sudden thought. "So where have you stayed?"

"Mama and the babies in the Altgelts' smoke-house and I with Etta. But *Herr* Altgelt is trying to find a better place."

As Papa lay back, a sad smile came to his lips. "Of course, I should have known already. Good old Ernst."

Late in the afternoon we started up and did not stop until we came to the ruins of our house after dark. I dismounted and stood beside Papa. He sat, staring at the ghostly shapes in the moonlight.

After a time he said, "The paintings?"

"Gone, Papa."

Another long silence.

"I will paint more, Sophie."

I put my face down into my hands. "Oh Papa, I should have tried to save the ..." My throat tightened and I could not say homestead scene.

He held out his arms and I went to him.

"*Nein*, Sophie, you had to make a choice, and there was only one. You know that surely."

I nodded. "But the homestead scene ..."

"I will paint another one, just as it remains in my head. So we will never forget."

I could not speak.

"Then, when the war is over, we'll build a new home on this very place. I promise."

I straightened up and looked at the lonely stone walls. The tightness in my throat gave way to tears that ran freely down my cheeks.

"How little we know what is in store for us when we are young, Sophie—both *gut* and bad. We think everything will always be like it is, never changing."

"I know better now, Papa."

"*Ja*, you know better now. You are not my *kleine* Sophie anymore. You are all grown up, and that is how it should be, how it must be."

I said nothing for a time. Then I dabbed away my tears with my skirt. "Does that make you sad, Papa?"

"Sad and glad at the same time. Like the ending of one story and the beginning of another."

I tried to smile, but my lips quivered.

"I thought about a lot of things when I lay in the chaparral," he went on. "About the killing. About my friends lying dead and the buzzards circling overhead. Once a buzzard landed near me and waddled around, waiting for me to die so he could peck my flesh to the bone."

I took his hand. "Stop, Papa."

"That's just what I did. I made myself stop and think about all of you instead. It kept me alive." He squeezed my hand. "I thought about how I want to see that you get the education you deserve, Sophie. The best place is Ursuline Academy in San Antonio. Even if it is Catholic."

I caught my breath. "Oh Papa, is it possible?"

"Anything is possible when this war is over."

We were silent for a time while I pondered the idea. Going to school in San Antonio, becoming a writer, seeing the world ... with Eduard?

"Do you think Eduard is alive?" I asked.

"It's surely possible, Sophie." Papa smiled. "Shall we move on now?"

"I like that idea, Papa."

We crossed Cypress Creek and came to the Altgelts' gate. Lamps shone in the windows, and someone stood at the front door, silhouetted against the light.

"Who is it?" *Herr* Altgelt called.

"Sophie and Papa," I answered.

Herr Altgelt turned. "Elisabet! It's Sophie and Friedrich!"

We heard a little scream and the sound of scraping chair legs. In a moment the doorway was filled with dark shapes rushing out to the gallery and across the yard, followed by *Tante* Emma carrying a lantern.

Willie was the first one out the gate. He had on little trousers and a shirt.

"Sophie!" he squealed. Then he stopped, staring at the travois and at Papa. "What happened to your leg?"

"Someone shot a little lead ball into it, Willie, but it's much better already."

"Is the ball still in there?"

"*Ja*, I decided to keep it." Papa grinned at Willie and held out his arms. "Just look at you—my *Männlein*. Come."

Willie flung himself into Papa's arms.

We were surrounded: Mama with Lena in her arms, *Tante* Emma, *Herr* Altgelt, and the children who ran about, squealing with excitement. Willie came to me then and raised his plump little arms. I picked him up and hugged him close.

When Lena began to cry, everyone stopped still. Mama and Papa stared at each other in silence. *Tante* Emma set the lantern down, took Lena from Mama's arms and patted her back, murmuring, "It's all right, Lena, your papa has come home."

Mama took a step toward the travois and hesitated. "Elisabet . . ." Papa said.

"*Mein lieber* Friedrich!" She rushed to his arms. "We thought that you . . ." She buried her face against his chest.

"I know, Elisabet, but I'm not. Thanks to Sophie."

In a moment Mama stood up and looked at me as if for the first time. "Why didn't you tell me then, Sophie?"

"I couldn't, Mama. I knew what you would say."

She came and embraced me.

"I hate to interrupt such a lovely scene," *Herr* Altgelt said, "but we must go inside. Our house could be under surveillance. You are not out of danger, Friedrich."

"*Ja*, Ernst, I know that surely."

Herr Altgelt, Mama, and I helped Papa out of the travois. With us on both sides, he hobbled into the house and stretched out on the sofa.

"I'll go for Doctor Pfeiffer," *Herr* Altgelt said. "We can trust him."

After he left, *Frau* Murck brought a bowl of

cottage cheese with honey which Mama fed Papa even though he could feed himself now.

"You know about our house, Friedrich?"

"*Ja*, Elisabet. I am just thankful that you and the babies are all right."

"I'm not a baby!" Willie said in his high–pitched voice. "I'm four years old now."

"*Ach*, of course, *Männlein*," said Papa. "You had a birthday while I was away."

Willie nodded.

"The Bremers have offered us the cabin behind their house," Mama went on. "We will be safe here in town until the war is over."

"That is very kind of them." Papa paused and took Mama's hand in his. I knew what he was about to say. "Elisabet, the Confederates are looking for sur-vivors. Duff has sworn to hang us all."

Mama's other hand flew to her mouth.

"You and the children go to the Bremers. I will stay here in the smokehouse, if Ernst and Emma will allow it, until my leg heals."

"Of course we will," *Tante* said.

"Then," Papa went on, "I have to leave for Mexico."

Mama shook her head slowly from side to side.

"*Ja*, Elisabet, it must be."

Mama stared at Papa for a moment. Then she embraced him.

Epilogue
Wednesday, November 12

It has been almost three months since I wrote because I have been saving these last pages for a momentous event. More about that later.

Papa's leg healed, although he walks with a limp. In a way it is a blessing because he won't be able to enlist. He hopes to get work with an illustrated weekly and do eyewitness battle drawings. Soldiers don't shoot artists, do they? Anyway, as Papa says, he never met an enemy at his easel.

While he was staying in the smokehouse, Mama sat for him. Since he had no paints, he did a pencil portrait. He took great care in shading so it looks like a black and white painting. But the best part is that they fell in love again.

Soon after Papa left in October, the news came that eight Germans, five of them from Comfort, had been shot and killed while trying to cross the Rio Grande. For a breathless moment I read the list of names—once, twice. But neither Papa nor Eduard were on it.

More and more men are leaving Comfort. Even

Herr Faltin. He left after a *Hängebande*, hanging gang, from Kerrville came to the store with bandanas over their faces. They would have hanged him, but he managed to hide just before they arrived. He is probably in Mexico by now. His wife is running the store. It seems we are becoming a village without men.

School commenced in September, and the war goes on. Who knows how long it will last? First one side wins a battle and then the other. In my opinion nobody wins. The *San Antonio Zeitung* reported a battle at Antietam Creek in the state of Maryland. Twenty–three thousand men lost their lives, and neither side won! In the midst of all this madness President Lincoln did something noble. He declared that all slaves are free forever.

In spite of the war, we carry on. Every day after school I go out to our homeplace and do my chores. Arlis drove some cattle to San Antonio and got a good price in gold. The rains returned in September. Before Papa left he had Arlis work the soil in our garden, and I planted peas, lettuce, cabbage, and onions with seeds that *Tante* Emma gave us. So we survive with help from our friends.

A norther swept in today, the first of the season. The wind is still thrashing the tree branches as I write. But my candle burns steadily, for this cabin is tightly chinked. It stands behind the Bremers' house on High Street. There is only one room with a gallery. I sit at our dining table before the fire. At the other end of the room Mama, Willie, and Lena are sleeping.

Now for the momentous event. After school I went to the store. Wonder of wonders! There were two letters from Mexico! One was addressed to Mama in Papa's hand. The other was for me from Eduard. I ran down Main to Sixth and up to High Street, words pounding in my head. Papa made it, Eduard is alive.

Willie was playing on the gallery with a little wooden boat that *Herr* Bremer carved for him.

"Willie . . . Papa made it!"

"I know."

Mama opened the door. She had Lena in her arms.

I held the letter out to her. "He made it, Mama. Papa is in Mexico."

She let out her breath as if she had been holding it ever since Papa left. Then, handing Lena to me, she opened the seal and began reading aloud. I will paste the letter on the next page.

Bagdad, Mexico
October 29, 1862

Meine Lieben!

I hope that you are all well. You will be relieved to know that I am safely across the Rio Grande. It was a long and arduous trip, but Fritz is surely a tireless horse. My leg is neither better nor worse. Still, I am happy to be alive, thanks to my brave girl.

In a few days I board a steamer that lies offshore even now. There are many of us taking passage to New Orleans, including one young man from Comfort. *Ja*, Sophie, I mean Eduard.

From there we will sail for New York. I am told that *Harper's Weekly* is looking for artists. So I have spent my time making some drawings to submit. Willie, here is a sketch of the steamer I shall soon board.

You may write to me in care of *Harper's Weekly* in New York. No hour passes that I do not think of you, Elisabet, Sophie, Willie, and *kleine* Lena. I embrace you and kiss you.

Yours,

Friedrich (Papa)

Willie came to see Papa's drawing. "Look," he said, "it has a smokestack just like mine."

"I see you have another letter, Sophie," Mama said.

"*Ja*, it's from Eduard."

She took Lena. "Go find a place to read it alone then."

I knew the perfect place. I hurried off to the creek crossing. The wind was cold, but I clutched my shawl close, holding the letter to my heart. At the creek I sat down beside Old Man Owl.

Carefully, so as not to tear the paper, I broke the seal and unfolded the letter. Here it is:

October 30, 1862

Liebe Sophie!

I hope that you have not forgotten me or the day we said *auf Wiedersehen*. I will surely never forget you or the day or Old Man Owl.

It is comforting to be here with your father as we prepare to sail for New York. He told me of your valiant journey to bring him home.

I feel lucky to be alive. Throughout my own journey I kept your gift of William Tell's words close to my heart. It helped me survive.

I will continue to look around with open eyes and trust in *Gott* and my own strength until this war is over. Then one day I will see you again.

Yours, Eduard

It is past midnight as I sit writing. I laid down my pen a little while ago and stepped out on the gallery. The north wind has cleared the sky to show a waning crescent moon. In a few days it will be only a sliver and then dark—waxing and waning until this war is over, and Papa and Eduard come home.

So I reach the end of my journal, dear reader. May you find it a hundred and fifty years from now and know that I, Anna Sophie Franziska Guenther, was here.

GERMAN WORDS

ach (ahkh)	alas
auf Wiedersehen (owf VEE-der-zayn)	goodbye
dank, danke (dahnk, DAHN-kuh)	thank you
Dummkopf (DOOM-kawpf)	dumbhead
Fachwerk (FAHKH-vehrk)	half–timber
Frau (frow)	Mrs.
Fräulein (FROY-line)	Miss
Freund (froynd)	friend
Gott (gawt)	God
Gott sei Dank (gawt zee dahnk)	thank God
Grossmutter (GROSS-moot-ter)	grandmother
Grossvater (GROSS-fah-ter)	grandfather
gut, guter (goot, GOOT-er)	good
gute Nacht (GOO-tuh nahkht)	good night
guten Abend (GOO-ten AH-bent)	good evening
guten Morgen (GOO-ten MOR-gen)	good morning
guten Tag (GOO-ten tahk)	good day
Hängebande (HAHNG–guh-bahnd)	hanging gang
Häuschen (HOY-shen)	little (out)house
Herr (hehr)	Mr.
Himmel (HIM-mehl)	heaven
Hund (hoont)	dog, hound
im (ihm)	in
ja (yah)	yes

jawohl (yah-VOHL)	yes indeed
Kinder (KIN-der)	children
kleine (KLINE-uh)	little
Kochkäse (KOHKH-kay-suh)	cooked cheese
Liebchen (LEEB-chin)	little love
Liebe (LEEB-uh)	love
Mädchen (MAYD-chen)	girl, maiden
Männlein (MEHN-line)	little man
mein, meine (mine, MINE-uh)	my
Milch (milch)	milk
nein (nine)	no
Pummelchen (PUHM-mehl-chin)	fat little girl
sehr (zehr)	very
Tannenbaum (TAHN-nen-baum)	fir tree
Tante (TAHN-tuh)	aunt
und (oont)	and
Weihnachtsmann (VIGH-nahkhts-mahn)	Santa Claus
Wildfang (VILT–fahng)	tomboy
wunderbar (VOON-dehr-bar)	wonderful
Zeitung (TSIGH-toong)	newspaper

243

ENGLISH WORDS

fidibus (FID-ih-bus)	a long, narrow piece of wood used for lighting lamps
gibbous moon (GIB-bus)	more than half full but less than full
reticule (RET-ih-kyool)	a woman's small purse

AUTHOR'S NOTE

The War Between the States, or the Civil War as we call it now, caused a terrible loss of lives. Did we really have to kill each other to keep this country together?

President Abraham Lincoln said, "A house divided against itself cannot stand." What, then, divided the North and the South? Most important was slavery. The northern states had become industrial and needed no slaves while the southern states remained agricultural and thought slaves were necessary to run the plantations.

The highly educated, idealistic German immigrants who settled in Texas could not abide the enslavement of human beings. Nor did they want their country divided. Thus, the Germans sided with the North and became an island of Unionists surrounded by stormy Confederate waters.

On this island Sophie wrote her journal. The words are hers, for I became Sophie. It seemed quite natural since my ancestors left Germany and came to Texas about the same time the Guenthers did. The only difference is that my ancestors were peasants while Sophie's parents were from an elite, educated society.

What makes us alike is that my father did not stay in the family ranching business. He became a professor of German language and literature at Southern Methodist University in Dallas and, in his own way, a Freethinker. I grew up in a cultured household with music and books, just as Sophie did. My father was not an artist like Papa, but my husband Tom is an illustrator, painter, and architect. Like Sophie I keep a journal that I hope someone will read a hundred and fifty years from now and know that I was here. And like Sophie, I once lost a journal, but unlike her, I never found it.

All the places in the story are real. I have used the German spelling of Friedrichsburg for Fredericksburg, as it came to be called. There is no connection between the name of the town and Papa's name, Friedrich.

Although Sophie's family is fictional, many of the characters are real: Ernst and Emma Altgelt, *Herr* Faltin, Captain Duff, Caspar and Emilie Real, Ernst Kramer, Doctor Pfeiffer, *Herr* Steves, and even *Herr* Schimmelpfennig, who did sit in a saddle on a liveoak branch and play his violin while people danced.

The historical background of Sophie's journal is fact. There was a Vigilance Committee of ruffians who rode about Central Texas terrorizing German Unionists. The Nueces River Massacre really happened, and those who escaped the battle were hanged on the spot if found.

Today a white stone shaft stands proudly in

Comfort, inscribed with the names of the men who were killed for being loyal to the Union. It is their gravesite, for their remains were brought back to Comfort after the war was over.

On August 10, 1996, Tom and I attended the 130th Anniversary and Rededication of this *Treue der Union* Monument which had been restored for the occasion. In my own journal I wrote:

> The ceremony began at nine o'clock in the morning while the air was still fresh. People gathered under the great liveoak that grows beside the monument. A hand bell was rung and each man's name was called. As I listened, I wondered if people would ever learn not to make war.

The next day we traveled to the Nueces River, following Sophie's journey. At the river I picked up a pebble, just as she did.

I have made many visits to the small town of Comfort, where people welcomed me with open arms. The best of times was when I spent a week in the Faltin House, a bed and breakfast apartment above Faltin & Company. Built on the same site as the earlier store, it is owned by August Faltin, the great-grandson of the original owner. Just below the windows of the spacious apartment stands the log and stone Faltin house, the model for Sophie's house. I could gaze at it while having breakfast of French toast covered with slices of baked cinnamon apples.

During that week I spent entire days absorbing the sights and sounds and smells of Comfort and the countryside. I watched the sun rise over Cypress Creek and found Old Man Owl at the crossing. I watched a flock of sheep grazing in the meadow below Sophie's homestead, listened to the wind sough in the liveoak branches, and felt myself becoming Sophie.

ILLUSTRATOR'S NOTE

Illustrators should draw, not write. But remembering that there was once a time when drawing and writing were one, I will give it a try.

I grew up watching my mother paint in our Seattle home, which inspired me to spend long hours drawing at my desk in the dormer window of my bedroom. In school I was sometimes punished, sometimes rewarded for drawing in class. I cartooned for my high school newspaper, but during Career Day an architect inspired me with his beautiful renderings to choose architecture. I studied and began careers in both art and architecture.

During our yearlong "Honeymoon Hobos" journey around the world, Janice and I began our first writer-illustrator partnership. I illustrated articles we each wrote about our travel observations for the Tokyo *Asahi Shimbun* and the *Texas Architect*.

When Janice wrote her first children's book, *A Paradise Called Texas*, our sons, Karl and Daniel, and I became an illustrator team. We continued with her *Texas Trilogy* until the boys moved on toward their careers, making movies. Many books later, Janice and I continue our partnership.

Images come from many sources while I am illustrating our books. Portraits by nineteenth-century German Texan artist Richard Petri and seventeenth-century Dutch artist Jan Vermeer, as well as a photograph of twelve-year-old Janice, inspired my portrait of Sophie on the cover. Incidentally, we purchased the marbled paper in a small shop in Venice. My creation of Papa's political cartoons was inspired by those of Thomas Nast, who did his best work during the Civil War. I also drew Eduard's Parthenon like an aspiring architect might have done it. Janice added the drawings that Sophie made of the house plan, Old Man Owl, and her journey map.

Janice and I confer about every stage of bookmaking from story idea to illustrations. We find this close collaboration stimulating.

THANKS WITH ALL MY HEART TO:

PAUL BURRIER, who knows more about the Nueces River Massacre than anyone in the world and loves to share his knowledge.

AUGUST FALTIN, for letting me use his great-grandfather's house as the model for Sophie's home.

CLEMENS AND ADELHEID HEINEN, for letting me roam the land and absorb the site that I chose for the Guenthers' homestead.

JEAN HESS, for opening her house on that site.

GILBERT JORDAN, my father, for a poetic translation of *William Tell* and for introducing me to books and music and the universe.

GREGORY KRAUTER, for giving me a headful of information about Comfort's history and its people. May his Ingenhuett Store rise from the ashes like the Phoenix.

GERLINDE LEIDING, for loaning me her German-English dictionaries and consulting on German usage.

VIRGINIA MESSER, my publisher and book designer extraordinaire, for making the cover more beautiful than I could imagine.

GUSTA B. NANCE, who read passages of *The Iliad* to my comparative literature class at Southern Methodist University with spinsterish fervor.

251

EMILIE REAL NEILL, for showing me Caspar Real's cabin and answering many questions about her ancestors.

IDA INGENHUETT PERKINS AND ROY PERKINS, for making me feel at home in Comfort and for telling me about the mockingbird.

LENA SHEFELMAN, my granddaughter, for reading the manuscript and giving me her thoughts.

RAY AND JAN WEEKS, who make the world's best French toast.

NOVELLA WILEY, for helping me with Latin and for teaching my son Daniel at Austin High School.

VALERIE WOOLVIN, for her warm hospitality in Sisterdale.

J. S.

CREDITS

Excerpts of *Wilhelm Tell* by Johann Cristoph Friedrich von Schiller are from a translation by Gilbert J. Jordan, pages 92 and 195. The Bobbs–Merrill Co. 1964.

Excerpt of *The Iliad* by Homer is from a translation by Lang, Leaf, and Myers. Included in *An Anthology of World Literature*, page 16. The Macmillan Co. 1946.

Excerpt of *To the Moon* by Johann Wolfgang von Goethe is adapted from a translation by John S. Dwight. Included in *The Permanent Goethe*, page 3. The Dial Press. 1948.

Excerpt of *Slovenly Peter* (*Der Struwwelpeter* by Heinrich Hoffmann) is a loose translation by Janice Shefelman.

The 23rd Psalm is from *The Holy Bible*, Authorized or King James Version, pages 636–637. The John C. Winston Co.

My Journey

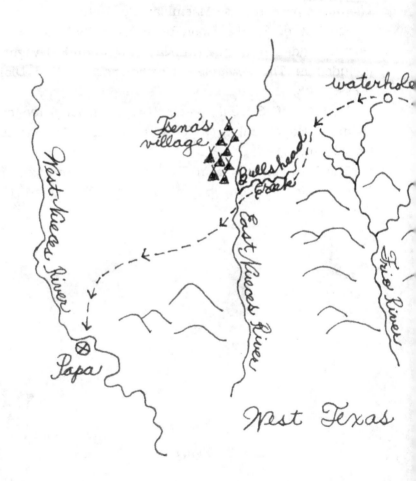

waterhole

Tsena's village

Bullshead Creek

West Nueces River

East Nueces River

Frio River

Papa

West Texas

Friedrichsburg
Pedernales River
North Fork
Guadalupe
Cypress Creek
South Fork
Turtle Creek
Comfort
Real cabin
River
Medina River
Sabinal River
Wilderness
N
E
S

RELATED BOOKS BY THE AUTHOR

A Paradise Called Texas
TEXAS BLUEBONNET AWARD NOMINEE

Willow Creek Home

Spirit of Iron

These three novels, The Texas Trilogy, are based on stories of the author's German ancestors. Mina, her great aunt, was a young girl in 1845 when they left Germany and came to Texas. Unlike Sophie's family, Mina's parents were not educated in German universities. They were peasants who came seeking a paradise but found hardship, tragedy, and adventure.

Comanche Song
BEST BOOK FOR THE TEEN AGE
THE NEW YORK PUBLIC LIBRARY

This novel tells the story of Sophie's friend, Chief Tsena, when he was a boy in 1840, the year white man changed his life forever. It is based on two historical encounters between the Comanches and Texans: the Council House Massacre and the Battle of Plum Creek.

For more information visit www.Shefelmanbooks.com